THE RESISTANCE TO POETRY

THE RESISTANCE TO POETRY

James Longenbach

THE UNIVERSITY OF CHICAGO PRESS
Chicago & London

JAMES LONGENBACH is the Joseph Henry Gilmore Professor of English
at the University of Rochester and the author of four distinguished critical stud-
ies of modern literature, most recently *Modern Poetry after Modernism*. His two
books of poems, *Threshold* and *Fleet River,* are published by the University of
Chicago Press.

The University of Chicago Press, Chicago 60637
The University of Chicago Press, Ltd., London
© 2004 by The University of Chicago
All rights reserved. Published 2004
Printed in the United States of America

13 12 11 10 09 08 07 06 05 04   1 2 3 4 5

ISBN: 0-226-49249-4 (cloth)

Library of Congress Cataloging-in-Publication Data

Longenbach, James.
    The resistance to poetry / James Longenbach.
        p. cm.
    Includes bibliographical references and index.
    ISBN 0-226-49249-4 (alk. paper)
    1. American poetry—21st century—History and criticism—Theory, etc.
  2. Poetry—History and criticism—Theory, etc.   I. Title.

PS325.L67   2004
809.1—dc22
                                                    2003019689

♾ The paper used in this publication meets the minimum requirements of the
American National Standard for Information Sciences—Permanence of Paper for
Printed Library Materials, ANSI Z39.48-1992.

Elli givan dinanzi, e io soletto
di retro, e ascoltava i lor sermoni,
ch'a poetar mi davano intelletto.

The marvel is to me how people read so much of it.

— JOHN KEATS

CONTENTS

PREFACE

THIS BOOK IS ABOUT the ways in which poetry is its own best enemy. For centuries, poems have resisted themselves more strenuously than they have been resisted by the culture receiving them. Their language is the language of self-questioning—metaphors that turn against themselves, syntax that moves one way because it threatens to move another, voices that speak because they are shattered. Poets who embrace these aspects of language are inevitably schooled in the art of self-resistance, and they consequently tend to recoil from any exaggeration of the cultural power of writing poems. At their most brazen, these poets have erred on the side of underestimating their art, aware that to exaggerate the extent of poetry's purchase on our attention is to weaken it. Some poets have hidden themselves in broad daylight. Others have been liberated by the marginality of poetry to explore strange ideas.

The book's first chapter looks at the ways in which poets since the time of Callimachus have resisted their own usefulness. The state of poetry today is the chapter's ultimate focus, and subsequent chapters examine a wide array of poets writing in the twenty-first century: Frank Bidart, Louise Glück, Jorie Graham, Michael Palmer, Carl Phillips, Charles Wright, and many others. Along the way, these chapters often look back to poets of the nineteenth and twentieth centuries; occasionally, earlier poets loom large as do writers of prose fiction and philosophy. Formal strategies associated with recent poetry are often shown to have been part of a poet's tool kit for centuries.

The chapters themselves are not organized around particular writers, however, but around techniques of poetic self-resistance. "The End of the Line" is about the work performed by line in the strategic absence of meter. "Forms of Disjunction" examines the ways in which poems turn unpredictably, while "Song and Story" considers the seduction of poems that privilege sound over sense. "Untidy Activity" is about the equivocations of metaphor, and "The Spokenness of Poetry" shows how lyric poems interrogate the metaphor of their own voice. "The Other Hand" is about the work of syntax. And the penultimate chapter, "Leaving Things Out," considers the ways in which poems tend to resist their own subject matter.

Implicit throughout each of these chapters is the notion that we read for the resistance, not in spite of it. It would not be quite right to say that poems give us pleasure to the degree that they resist their own capacity to do so, for poetry's mechanisms of self-resistance are themselves the source of our pleasure. They are the means by which a great poem feels always about to be discovered, no matter how relevant its wisdom may or may not be. The book's final chapter, "Composed Wonder," argues that the resistance to poetry is quite specifically the wonder of poetry.

I have been writing this book for many years, and even when pieces of the argument have appeared elsewhere, they have changed radically as the shape of the book has become clearer. Parts of chapters 3, 4, 7, and 8 were originally published in *Raritan* (3, 7), *Salmagundi* (8), the *Southwest Review* (8), and the *Yale Review* (4), and I am grateful for the ongoing support of the editors of these magazines. Other chapters were delivered as lectures in the Warren Wilson College MFA Program or at the Bread Loaf Writers' Conference, and I am also grateful for the responses of people who listened. Kenneth Gross, Edward Hirsch, Robert Pinsky, and Joanna Scott attended to the manuscript. Other debts are acknowledged on every page following this one.

THE RESISTANCE TO POETRY

I. *The Resistance to Poetry*

IMAGINE A COUNTRY in which poetry matters because by definition poems are relevant to daily life. It would not be a large, flat country that nobody wants to visit; it would be a small island brimming with natural beauty but lacking natural resources. The inhabitants of the island would feel at every second that they are not in control of their own destiny; the language they speak is not their own. At the same time, their sense of what might constitute an indigenous culture is unmanageably complex, obscured by centuries of internal strife.

"Do not be elected to the Senate of your country," said the Irish poet William Butler Yeats to the American poet Ezra Pound. It was one of the sweetest remarks Yeats ever made, for while an Irish poet was appointed to the Senate of the newly constituted Irish state in 1922, no poet would ever be elected to the Senate of the United States. Many American poets have coveted the relevance Yeats could take for granted, and some have berated themselves for writing as if history happened somewhere else; others have addressed the most pressing issues and events of their time. But the marginality of poetry is in many ways the source of its power, a power contingent on poetry's capacity to resist itself more strenuously than it is resisted by the culture at large.

Poets have been on the defensive at least since the time of Plato, and rightly so, since philosophers and literary critics have distrusted poetry. But poems do not necessarily ask to be trusted. Their language revels in duplicity and disjunction, making it difficult for us to assume that any particular poetic gesture is inevitably responsible or irresponsible to the culture that gives the language meaning: a poem's obfuscation of the established terms of accountability might be the poem's most accountable act—or it might not. Distrust of poetry (its potential for inconsequence, its pretension to consequence) is the stuff of poetry. And the problem with many defenses of poetry is the refusal to recognize that the enemy lies within.

It has lain there for a long time. In the third century B.C.E. the Greek poet Callimachus refused the Homeric challenge of writing an epic narrative, preferring to write small poems about love rather than poems aspiring to a great deal of cultural weight. "Not I but Zeus owns the thunder," said Callimachus to critics who complained that he was ignoring his civic duties.

> When I first put a tablet on my knees, the Wolf-God
>   Apollo appeared and said:
> "Fatten your animal for sacrifice, poet,
>   but keep your muse slender."

Apollo's reprimand was extremely influential. The story echoed in the pastoral landscape of Virgil's sixth eclogue ("A Shepherd / Should feed fat sheep and sing a slender song"), and it echoed again in Propertius, whose elegies were updated by Ezra Pound. "You idiot," says Apollo to the poet, "What are you doing with that water: / Who has ordered a book about heroes?"

By the time Pound adapted these lines in 1917, justifying his antipathy toward poets who were eager to take up the epic challenge of the Great War, Apollo's reprimand had become a venerable topos, one invoked even by poets whose more programmatic defenses of poetry might seem to belie it. Yeats had recently made the Callimachian refusal in "On Being Asked for a War Poem," and W. H. Auden would make it even more bluntly in his elegy for Yeats: "poetry makes nothing happen." More recently, Callimachus's call for a "slender muse" has appeared as the epigraph to Harryette Mullen's *Muse & Drudge*, a book that advertises the possibility that its playful, pun-laden poems may not be performing the heavy-lifting cultural work associated with the epic. "Blurred rubble slew of vowels / stutter war no more," says Mullen, who makes us wonder if she stutters to a purpose: are her disturbances of "the natural order of things" merely the "ruses of a lunatic muse"? An unequivocal answer to this question won't be found. The point is that poets tend to be suspicious of their own designs, forcing their best discoveries against the wall of their limitations.

Of course poets have not done this consistently, and some poets have mustered the effort rarely if at all. Upbraiding Shelley, Pound once said that poets ought to be acknowledged legislators. And Yeats certainly aspired to set statesmen right when his attention was turned toward Ireland rather than toward what he perceived as England's war. What's more, as the notoriety of Auden's elegy for Yeats suggests, there can be a romance to the refusal of romance, a weightiness to the spurning of unearned weight. "The best I had done seem'd to me blank and suspicious," admitted Whitman; but rather than thwarting the desire to contain multitudes, doubt fuels the drama of ambition. If poetry is the resistance to poetry, what prevents poetry from assuming the mantle of its own greatness by virtue of its long-practiced ambition to drop it? Does dropping the mantle in Belfast mean the same thing as dropping the mantle in Brooklyn?

Imagine a country where great political leaders not only expect but regularly receive poems celebrating their achievements as well. Poems that are read immediately for their relevance but also cherished for centuries thereafter. A place where poetic achievement is so highly valued, poetic skill so desirable, that some leaders even write their own celebratory poems. This place was Augustan Rome: this pressure was what made an Augustan poet's invocation of Callimachus weighty, no matter how ritualized the gesture became. "Now everyone / Is seized with the desire to write a poem," said Horace in his epistle to Augustus, whom he advises to "know exactly / Whom you're choosing to tend the temple of / Your deeds of peace and war." Horace takes pains to recuse himself. "I'd much prefer to be able to be the teller / Of tales of heroic deeds," he admits,

> But the grandeur of your deeds is out of scale
> For such poetry as mine; and my self-knowledge
> Keeps me from trying for more than I have the strength for.

Horace did celebrate the achievements of his emperor within the smaller compass of the odes; his humility is belied by skill. But his skill is pointedly Callimachian, his true subject the epic encounters between young lovers rather than the epic as such.

If the assumption of poetry's relevance can be oppressive to poets, the assumption of its irrelevance can be liberating, especially when a culture threatens either to foreclose or to exaggerate a poem's potential for subversiveness. When Thomas Hardy grew weary of writing novels that aroused distracting controversy, he turned to poems because he knew that their revelations would be accorded less attention: "If Galileo had said in verse that the world moved," he said, "the Inquisition might have let him alone." The implications of Hardy's poems are at least as threatening as those of his novels, just as Horace's praise of Augustus is no less elaborate for being tucked away in the fourth book of the odes. But by writing poems, Hardy was released from the pressure of notoriety to be more resolutely idiosyncratic. He embraced a medium that succeeds by exploiting rather than suppressing the inevitable tendency of language to resist its own utility. To harness the cultural marginality of poetry was the next step, and a wide variety of poets, living in places more like Brooklyn than Rome, have taken it.

"I do not appear," wrote Marianne Moore to Pound when he asked where her poems were being published. Like Pound, Moore made Callimachian gestures when other poets were eager to celebrate the Great War, but her gestures seem less compromised: can there be an arrogance to the act of dropping the mantle of poetry's greatness if nobody sees you do it? Moore neglected no opportunity to make her poems seem easily underestimable. She diminished the bravura of her intricately designed syllabic stanzas, calling them "an arrangement of lines and rhymes that I liked." Eventually the syllabics seemed to her unaccountably showy, and from 1921 until 1925, when she stopped writing poetry for several years, Moore adopted a plain-spoken, mostly end-stopped free verse. She described "Marriage," her most astonishing free-verse poem, as nothing but "statements that took my fancy which I tried to arrange plausibly."

> The blue panther with black eyes,
> the basalt panther with blue eyes,
> entirely graceful—
> one must give them the path—
> the black obsidian Diana
> who "darkeneth her countenance
> as a bear doth,"

the spiked hand
that has an affection for one
and proves it to the bone,
impatient to assure you
that impatience is the mark of independence,
not of bondage.
"Married people often look that way."

In this passage from "Marriage," Moore quotes from a 1609 translation of Ecclesiasticus ("The wickedness of woman changeth her face: and she darkeneth her countenance as a bear, and sheweth it like sackcloth"), but she adjusts the context, making Diana's ursine face reflect not her essential wickedness but the threat of the institution of marriage. Does this fervor enter the poem in spite of Moore's effort to diminish the poem's purchase on our attention or because of it? Is her inconsequence of manner due to a failure of nerve or to a strategic appraisal of the unpredictable ways in which the language of poetry may (or may not) discover its relevance over time?

Indisputable answers to these questions would depend on whether the poem were read in Rome or Brooklyn—in a place where poetry is by and large respected or dismissed. "In choosing his manner of death," said Nadezhda Mandelstam of her husband's decision to write a poem mocking Stalin, "M. was counting on one remarkable feature of our leaders: their boundless, almost superstitious respect for poetry." Mandelstam's own respect for poetry was more fruitfully equivocal, but he did not have the freedom to indulge in poetry's penchant for equivocation; unlike Hardy's Galileo, he lived in a country where respect for poetry helped to erode the liberties a poet might otherwise hope to preserve. Nadezhda Mandelstam's clear sense that her husband *chose* his manner of death, counting on his culture's respect for poetry, is all the more unsettling when we remember that Mandelstam's poem about the "Kremlin mountaineer" is, like many poems, a little collection of fanciful metaphors: "the ten thick worms of his fingers," "the huge laughing cockroaches on his top lip."

Imagine a country in which poetry is respected as never before. A country that supports almost 300,000 Web sites devoted to poetry. A country in which the eighth most popular term plugged into Internet search engines is poetry (edging out football, Beanie Babies, and the Bible). A country in which a poet appears on the front page of its most prestigious newspaper because of the unprecedented size of the advance against royalties he received from his publisher. A country in which another poet's dismay over the gift of one hundred million dollars to a monthly literary magazine is said to betray a patronizing attitude toward the art.

This country is of course the United States in the twenty-first century. It's difficult to complain about poetry's expanding audience, but it's more difficult to ask what a culture that wants poetry to be popular wants poetry to be. The audience has by and large been purchased at the cost of poetry's inwardness: its strangeness, its propensity to defeat its own expectations, its freedom to explore new (or old) linguistic avenues without necessarily needing to worry about economic success. The crucial events in the history of poetry make millions of dollars seem beside the point, but it is difficult to celebrate such events, even if we're able to recognize their importance while they're happening. Nor do they necessarily need to be celebrated. "If we are to save poetry," said Richard Howard in an excoriation of National Poetry Month, " . . . we must restore poetry to that status of seclusion and even secrecy that characterizes only our authentic pleasures." "Poetry is part of our shared, communal life," responded Robert Pinsky. That is certainly the case, but the force of Howard's point lingers because we can never quite be sure what constitutes our communal life, especially as it changes over time. The fact that football, Beanie Babies, or even novels are part of that life does not mean that poetry will preoccupy us in similarly meaningful ways.

Howard's point also lingers because it has been made as long as there have been poets to make it—as long, that is, as a culture has expected poems to fulfill prescribed functions rather than discover their relevance. It is "foreign to my thought, as Firmament to Fin," said Emily Dickinson when Thomas Higginson suggested that she delay publishing her poems until they were rid of their unruly rhythms and rhymes. In ways less obviously imbricated in communal life, however, Dickinson did publish her poems. She included hundreds of them in letters; she bound many more of them together with string to make the booklets we've come to call fascicles. Were these the strategies of a poet defeated by the literary culture of her time or of a poet unwilling to bend to its prescriptions?

At times Dickinson's isolation seems aggressively chosen, but at other times the dilemma seems more interestingly ambiguous. If "Best Things dwell out of Sight," as one poem begins, then how may best things be described?

> Most shun the Public Air
> Legitimate, and Rare—
>
> The Capsule of the Wind
> The Capsule of the Mind
>
> Exhibit here, as doth a Burr—
> Germ's Germ be where?

We are able to conceive of what is hidden in these lines because we are able to perceive what is visible. The capsule of the mind (the body) is as plainly apprehendable as the burr, and we assume the existence of the germ just as we assume the existence of the mind. The more exquisite "Germ's Germ" is conceivable because we may split the burr to see the germ, and even the daringly intangible metaphor of the "Capsule of the Wind" is explicable because it is followed by the more readily imagined "Capsule of the Mind." Yet the poem is thrilling because the point of these metaphors remains partially occluded: the metaphors oscillate between allowing us to picture an image (the body) and tempting us with the unpicturable (the wind's container).

"In the artist of all kinds," said the psychoanalyst D. W. Winnicott, "one can detect an inherent dilemma, which belongs to the co-existence of two trends, the urgent need to communicate and the still more urgent need not to be found." The artist merely makes this tension manifest, since for Winnicott the human psyche is divided between a need to be known and the need to remain forever occluded. It is "a sophisticated game of hide-and-seek," and a game impossible to win. For if "it is a joy to be hidden," says Winnicott with a gnomic confidence worthy of Dickinson, it is "disaster not to be found." Concealed in the concluding question of "Best Things dwell out of

Sight" is a possibility that feels both threatening and enticing: if we could picture the "Capsule of the Wind," then the "Germ's Germ" ought to *beware*.

A poet's desire to sequester herself could seem alternately arrogant and precious, but it could also be liberating—the creation of a space in which a poem may be pushed to extremes the culture wouldn't know how to purchase or ignore. The literary culture of Dickinson's day could not accommodate her unruly rhythms and idiosyncratic punctuation, which were regularized by her first editors. Her equally expressive lineation continues to be regularized today, though the nature of its importance is often debated. As Dickinson set them down, the final lines of "Best Things dwell out of Sight" looked like this.

> Most shun the
> Public Air
> Legitimate, and Rare—
>
> The Capsule of the
> Wind
> The Capsule of the
> Mind
>
> Exhibit here, as
> doth a burr—
> Germ's Germ be where?

For ears educated by Milton or Williams, Dickinson's line endings function aurally: the poet who employs punctuation with no grammatical function in order to create pauses and stresses that run against meter ("You almost pitied—it—you—it worked so—") also harnesses the tension between syntax, meter, and line to control the rhythmic life of her poems: "The Capsule of the / Wind / The Capsule of the / Mind." But some readers will always maintain that Dickinson's line endings are simply produced by the collision of handwriting and margin, just as earlier readers maintained that her punctuation would have been corrected had she published her poems in conventional ways. Rather than diminishing the power of Dickinson's achievement, however, such doubts are essential to it: her poems are so strange, so shockingly themselves, that no fully programmatic account of them could ever be mustered.

Comments on Dickinson's relationship to the literary culture of her time are inevitably speculative, but inasmuch as all poets render themselves simultaneously hidden and found, Dickinson engineered highly idiosyncratic versions of familiar methods. Her poems became part of shared, communal life because she preserved a status of seclusion and even of secrecy. To ignore the nagging possibility that Dickinson may not have been in complete control of this dialectic is to ignore the tenuousness of any poem's claim on our attention. To ignore the tenuousness is to undermine the claim's power, to forget that we enjoy what we find because it was hidden. A literary culture that celebrates poetry's availability at the expense of its inwardness would ultimately become a place in which poetry finds no place to hide, no home.

Imagine having no place to hide. You are carrying a heavy burden, and you have a long way to go. But the hills around you are furred in green, and in the distance the snow-capped tips of the Carpathian mountains emerge from the clouds. Lines from a poem drift into your consciousness—lines that speak intimately of your burden. Something comes, then nothing. Just before you reach your destination, the poem's final lines appear as if by magic in your mouth. "For a moment," you say to your companion, "I forget who I am and where I am."

Primo Levi tells this story in *If This Is a Man,* his account of the ten months he endured at Auschwitz. Having spent the morning scraping the inside of an underground gas tank, Levi is selected to walk half a mile to retrieve the heavy soup pot for his Kommando; the poem he tries to remember is the Ulysses canto of the *Inferno.* "Consider well your seed," says Ulysses to his men: "You were not born to live as a mere brute does, // But for the pursuit of knowledge and the good." These lines induce in Levi a feeling of self-forgetfulness, yet their wisdom is far from consoling. For inasmuch as Ulysses's desire to transcend his brutish existence recalls Levi's desire, the parallel is darkened by the spectacular failure of Ulysses's quest: he sees the mountain of Purgatory looming before him but drowns with all his men before reaching the destination. Similarly, Levi's journey ends when he returns to his Kommando with the soup pot, and a language of terminal reality replaces a language of possibility.

> *"Kraut und Rüben? Kraut und Rüben."* The official announce-
> ment is made that the soup today is of cabbages and turnips:
> *"Choux et navets. Kaposzta és répak."*
>
> *"And over our heads the hollow seas closed up."*

Levi ends his own story with the final line of the Ulysses canto: the two journeys end in oblivion, and the inability of the poem to do anything about human suffering is poignantly clear. How did Dante's poem matter to Levi?

Levi initially recalls the Ulysses canto in order to teach his companion, a young Frenchman, a few words of Italian. He remembers several lines, then stops; he recalls a later line and tries to connect one passage to the other by reconstructing the rhyme scheme. He realizes with satisfaction that the Italian *misi me* (I set forth) does not match precisely the French *je me mis*—"it is much stronger and more audacious, it is a chain that has been broken, it is a throwing oneself on the other side of a barrier." This process, one word leading to another, qualifying another, is what consoles Levi. For a moment, he is rescued from the narratives of utility that structure every second of his life: the poem's language creates an interior space where for a moment he may hide. But at the end of the journey, Levi is plummeted back into a world in which utility is all, a world in which words cannot resist themselves because the German, French, and Polish words for "cabbages and turnips" refer perfectly and interchangeably to things. "For a moment I forget who I am and where I am," says Levi, and the phrase is powerful because it acknowledges that a poem's consolation is neither permanent nor complete.

A poem can't help but to be meaningful; it may speak as easily to one person as to a thousand. But especially when it has something urgent to say, a poem's power inheres less in its conclusions than in its propensity to resist them, demonstrating their inadequacy while moving inevitably toward them. At the same time, however, a poetry content with limitation would be merely as alluring as a poetry content with grandeur. Dickinson, Dante, Horace—these are not poets who shied away from their own strangeness, making poems that are easily consumed. Their poems are nourishing because of the fervor with which they confront themselves, harnessing the inevitable tendency of language to mean one thing because it threatens to mean another.

Poets fear wisdom. This is why great poems threaten to feel beside the point precisely when we want them to reflect our importance: language returns our attention not to confirm what we know but to suggest that we might be different from ourselves. We have only to write one poem to feel the possibility of never writing another. We have only to write the next poem to discover its inadequacy. To employ figurative language is to hear its implications slip away from us. To write in lines is to feel their control of intonation and stress beginning to waver. To discover one's true wildness is to feel the ghost of Callimachus bearing down. Still, these mechanisms of self-resistance are a gift, for without them we could not feel the wonder of poetry more than once. Nor could we rediscover our pleasure in the unintelligibility of the world. Imagine forgetting from second to second what we are for. Imagine a sense of vocation contingent on our need to remain unknown to ourselves. Rather than asking to be justified, poems ask us to exist.

II.   *The End of the Line*

LISTEN FIRST TO William Carlos Williams.

> The sunlight in a
> yellow plaque upon the
> varnished floor
>
> is full of a song
> inflated to
> fifty pounds pressure
>
> at the faucet of
> June that rings
> the triangle of the air
>
> pulling at the
> anemones in
> Persephone's cow pasture—
>
> When from among
> The steel rocks leaps
> J. P. M.
>
> who enjoyed
> extraordinary privileges
> among virginity
>
> to solve the core
> of whirling flywheels
> by cutting

the Gordian knot
with a Veronese or
perhaps a Rubens—

What is a line of poetry for? Throughout his 1923 volume *Spring and All,* Williams bends syntax relentlessly across the line, using enjambment to determine the placement of stress. Sometimes the enjambment throws emphasis on the beginning of the line ("The sunlight in a / yellow plaque"), sometimes on the end ("extraordinary privileges / among virginity"). Having capitalized on the tension between syntax and line, Williams logically prefers a shorter line, one narrow enough to exclude almost any suggestion of syntactical pattern ("varnished floor"; "the Gordian knot"; "J. P. M."). By holding us back, the line keeps us racing forward, hungry for predication.

Listen in contrast to Ezra Pound.

> The silver mirrors catch the bright stones and flare,
> Dawn, to our waking, drifts in the green cool light;
> Dew-haze blurs, in the grass, pale ankles moving.
> Beat, beat, whirr, thud, in the soft turf
>   under the apple-trees,
> Choros nympharum, goat-foot, with the pale foot alternate;
> Crescent of blue-shot waters, green-gold in the shallows,
> A black cock crows in the sea-foam.

By the time he wrote this passage from canto 4, Pound had discovered the free verse line that would sustain him for the next sixty years: unlike Williams, Pound almost never enjambs a line. The end of the line is usually coincident with a strong punctuation mark, and on the rare occasions when it is not, the line ending makes more emphatic the normative turn of syntax ("soft turf / under"). Having sacrificed all tension between syntax and line, Pound logically prefers a longer line, a line built from a variety of smaller units of syntax, a line that privileges its self-contained rhythmic pattern over the poem's forward momentum. And if the static quality of Pound's end-stopped line feels appropriate to his characteristic subject (the return of ancient spiritual presences to a timeless present), Williams's rush of blunt enjambments feels crucial to his: the threat of J. Pierpont Morgan's antiquarian taste to the promise of contemporary art's state of endless becoming.

"At a particular time, at a particular date, in a particular room," remembered Pound, "two authors, neither engaged in picking the other's pocket, decided that the dilution of *vers libre* . . . had gone too far and that some counter-current must be set going." The two authors were Pound and Eliot, the time around 1917. Modernist free verse had already entered its decadence, and the countercurrent was soon to appear in Pound's *Hugh Selwyn Mauberley* and Eliot's *Poems:* rhymed tetrameter quatrains. To put it negatively, a once revolutionary mode of writing had quickly become an orthodoxy, a set of stylistic prescriptions that might be harnessed as ineptly or as brilliantly as rhymed quatrains. But the negative judgment rests on the wonder of achievement: in just a few years free verse had become as supple and capacious an instrument as rhymed quatrains. Pound would of course go on to write a great deal of free verse, and, together with the other moderns, he bequeathed an enormously rich vocabulary to later poets, one that has needed to be continuously reinvented.

The rate at which we confront Williams's enjambments may feel overwhelming, but the nature of many of his line endings is not different from one variety of Milton's. For Satan, Milton explains in *Paradise Lost,* conscience "wakes the bitter memory / Of what he was, what is, and what must be"—or so we might conclude, stopping at what appears to be the end of the line; but the syntax continues: "Of what he was, what is, and what must be / Worse." This enjambment provides simultaneously the stillness of a completed clause and the thrill of discovering that the sentence moves on. When Milton explains how the story of Mulcibar has been told in the past, concluding with the phrase "thus they relate, / Erring," he describes the effect of his own line endings: the error becomes ours, the word "erring" surprising us because of its placement at the beginning of the line, the new line's expected iamb flipped into a trochee for additional emphasis.

Paradise Lost is of course a metered poem; our sense that we have come to the end of the line with "Of what he was, what is, and what must be" is emphasized by the thousands of pentameter lines we have read prior to this one. "The musick of the English heroick line," said Dr. Johnson in his life of Milton, "strikes the ear so faintly that it is easily lost, unless all the syllables of every line co-operate together; this co-operation can be only obtained by the preservation of every verse unmingled with another as a distinct system of sounds, and this distinctness is obtained and preserved by the artifice of rhyme." Without rhyme, Johnson ventured, only a very few readers can perceive where a blank verse line ends or begins. And without meter, early antagonists of free verse maintained, no one can perceive where the line ends or begins. By the same logic, early defenders claimed that we may identify a free verse line as such because in good free verse the line is a complete syntactical entity. Such logic will allow us to read Whitman or Pound but not Williams—not, at least, the Williams of *Spring and All.* Listen to the kind of free verse Williams was writing just a few years earlier.

I walk back streets
admiring the houses
of the very poor:
roof out of line with sides,
the yards cluttered
with old chicken wire, ashes,
furniture gone wrong;
the fences and outhouses
built of barrel-staves
and parts of boxes, all,
if I am fortunate,
smeared a bluish green
that properly weathered
pleases me best
of all colors.
         No one
will believe this
of vast import to the nation.

John Hollander has said that Milton's enjambments "annotate" his syntax; J. V. Cunningham once said that the kind of line endings Williams employs here in "Pastoral" merely "parse" the syntax. That is, while these lines are not end-stopped, they almost always follow the normative turns of syntax rather than cutting against syntax, annotating it with emphasis the syntax would not otherwise provide.

By the time Williams wrote "Pastoral" he had embraced his characteristic subject matter and diction (both strategically plain) but he had not discovered a way to make the poem embody his conviction that such plain things are indeed of vast import to the nation. Hence the poem's adamant closure—a gesture one never finds in *Spring and All*. Without the drama of discovery provided by more radically enjambed lines (a dynamic sense that we "relate, / Erring"), Williams must layer a sense of wonder over the poem's thematic content.

What changed Williams's prosody so radically in such a short time? Or, to put it another way, what allowed him to distinguish line from syntax in the absence of meter? It could not have been the example of early mentor, Ezra Pound, who had already settled into a rigorously end-stopped line. Listen to the 1918 version of Marianne Moore's "The Fish."

> *The Fish*
>
> Wade through black jade.
> Of the crow-blue mussel-shells, one
> Keeps adjusting the ash-heaps;
> Opening and shutting itself like
>
> An injured fan.
> The barnacles undermine the
> Side of the wave—trained to hide
> There—but the submerged shafts of the
>
> Sun, split like spun
> Glass, move themselves with spotlight swift-
> Ness into the cervices—
> In and out, illuminating . . .

This is not metered or free but syllabic verse: the four lines of each stanza contain (in order) four, eight, seven, and eight syllables. The first line, enjambed with the title, is end-stopped, as is the third, fifth, and eleventh line; the other lines range from the kind of radical enjambment Williams began to favor in *Spring and All* ("undermine the / Side") to more properly Miltonic enjambment ("trained to hide / There"). The poem is also rhymed—though not in a way that would have pleased Dr. Johnson, for the rhymes are located in positions that diffuse rather than enhance our ability to hear the end of the line. That is, in the first and third line of every stanza, the first word in the line rhymes with the last word in the line: "wade through black jade"; "Keeps adjusting the ash-heaps." In addition, the rhyming syllables are often strategically unaccented: "An injured fan"; "Ness into the crevices."

Listen in contrast to the 1919 version of "The Fish."

> wade
> through black jade.
>> Of the crow blue mussel shells, one
>>> keeps
>>> adjusting the ash heaps;
>> opening and shutting itself like
>
> an
> injured fan.
>> The barnacles which encrust the
>>> side
>>> of the wave, cannot hide
>> there; for the submerged shafts of the
>
> sun,
> split like spun
>> glass, move themselves with spotlight swift-
>>> ness
>>> into the crevices—
>> in and out, illuminating . . .

Moore altered only a few words of the poem, but she completely redesigned its syllabic organization in order to place her rhymes in conventional positions—at the end of the line. We now have six-line stanzas, lines of one, three, eight, one, six, and eight syllables, and a more clearly identifiable rhyme scheme (a, a, x, b, b, x). The result is that we hear the poem radically differently because the newly intro-duced enjambments force us to recognize the rhymes emphatically, encouraging us in turn to place strong accents on syllables we had been at greater liberty to neglect. The effect of the new enjambment of the first line ("wade / through black jade") is familiar from Frost's

"After Apple Picking," where meter and rhyme conspire to mark the end of the line emphatically: "Cherish in hand, lift down, and not let fall. / For all / That struck the earth." But the effect of "an / injured fan" or "spotlight swift- / ness / into the crevices" pushes a familiar principle to a fresh extreme, forcing us to stress unexpected syllables and slowing down the forward momentum of the poem. The new lineation has so drastically annotated the syntax that the poem sounds completely different.

Sounds—not just looks. It's true that Moore's syllabic patterns are in a sense for the eye, but even if the enjambments in "The Fish" or the poems of *Spring and All* are also seen, the effect of the line endings is registered aurally, and the aural effect is the raison d'être of the line. "By the tone of voice," said Moore in "The Accented Syllable," "I mean that intonation in which the accents which are responsible for it are so unequivocal as to persist, no matter under what circumstances the syllables are read or by whom they are read." Moore showed Williams how to use line endings to create that pattern of emphasis in the absence of a prosody that equated line with a consistent metrical unit, a regular syllable count, or even a self-contained unit of syntax.

> They taste good to her
> They taste good
> to her. They taste
> good to her

In this well-known passage from "To a Poor Old Woman," Williams offers a programmatic version of effects he achieves more subtly in the poems of *Spring and All:* line endings work against the forward motion of the repeated syntax, isolating particular words and forcing us to create a different pattern of emphasis with each repetition. Again, the effect as such is not unprecedented; consider Milton's deployment of enjambment within simple, mostly declarative syntax.

> Hell heard th' insufferable noise, Hell saw
> Heav'n ruining from Heav'n, and would have fled
> Affrighted.

The syntax (hell heard, hell saw, hell would have fled) is positioned within the pentameter line in three different ways, forcing us to alter the placement of stress within a repeated pattern of syntax. Meter (but not rhyme) helps to highlight the line's rhythmic identity in this case, but an unmetered line has its own identity once it is played against syntax. If we substitute Williams's little sentence for Milton's, the passage from *Paradise Lost* would read this way.

> They taste good to her. They taste
> good to her, and would have tasted
> good.

Think back to the literary-historical moment with which I began. By the time Pound and Eliot published their poems in rhymed quatrains, they would have witnessed the maturity of several distinct species of free verse line: Pound's relentlessly end-stopped line; the "annotating" line Williams was just beginning to employ; and the "parsing" line of "Pastoral." Add to these three the sort of free verse Eliot himself was writing (a line that invokes a regular meter in order to avoid it) as well as the highly discursive end-stopped free verse Marianne Moore was beginning to write, and we have an extremely sophisticated free verse vocabulary. What were Pound and Eliot objecting to?

The only poem I've examined that might have drawn down their wrath is Williams's "Pastoral"—not because it uses a parsing line but because it parses syntax so consistently that the poem cannot generate the energy required to make its own subject matter seem sufficiently worthy of notice. Stevens and H. D. also used a parsing line more often than not. But sometimes with a difference: listen to the opening lines of "The Snow Man."

> One must have a mind of winter
> To regard the frost and the boughs
> Of the pine-trees crusted with snow;
>
> And have been cold a long time
> To behold the junipers shagged with ice,
> The spruces rough in the distant glitter . . .

These lines parse the poem's single sentence, confirming rather than interrupting its drive toward predication. After the semicolon at the end of the first tercet, we feel the poem beginning again, invoking the power of the first line's auxiliary verb ("must"); we are reassured to find the same kind of line ending dividing the syntax in the same place. These endings highlight the parallel syntax, placing the infinitives "to regard" and "to behold" at the beginning of the second line of each tercet. Then, once the first two lines of the second tercet have repeated the pattern of the first tercet, we might expect the third lines to match up as well. But here Stevens introduces an apposition ("The spruces rough in the distant glitter"), delaying the expected "Of the" until the beginning of the third tercet: "The spruces rough in the distant glitter / Of the January sun." We are thrown just slightly off balance. We are thrown further when the repetition of the infinitive ("to regard," "to behold," "to think") appears not at the beginning but at the end of the line: "Of the January sun; and not to think." At this point, the poem takes off, leaving behind the steady reassurance of the parsing line for a line that annotates the increasingly hypotactic syntax with increasingly radical enjambment.

> Of the January sun; and not to think
> Of any misery in the sound of the wind,
> In the sound of a few leaves,
>
> Which is the sound of the land
> Full of the same wind
> That is blowing in the same bare place
>
> For the listener, who listens in the snow,
> And, nothing himself, beholds
> Nothing that is not there and the nothing that is.

Repeated words function in these lines the way rhymes function in "The Fish": while the syntax rushes forward, our ears are pulled back—first by the repetition of the word "sound," then by the repetition of "wind," and finally by the repetition of the word signifying repetition itself: "same." With each reoccurrence, these words relinquish some of their semantic power. We become less confidant of their meaning and more aware of their sound. We want to reconsider the earlier instance of the word, eager to understand the poem's discrimination of multiple meanings, but the syntax pushes ahead, its urgency reinforced by the increasingly radical enjambments ("the land / Full"; "beholds / Nothing"). We have heard the word "behold" earlier in the poem (matched up confidently with "regard"), but when it appears dangling at the end of the poem's penultimate line, about to introduce the poem's most discriminating repetition ("nothing" from "nothing"), it has become a different word, a word that demands a different mode of understanding: the poem's semantic conundrum has been fueled by an increasing tension between syntax and line.

"Stevens's line is shaped syntactically," says Donald Justice, thinking more of the first half of "The Snow Man" than the second: "that is, it stops at the end of a phrase or clause and does not break across the phrase or contrary to it." In contrast, Justice continues, thinking more of the Williams of *Spring and All* than of "Pastoral," the "Williams line was more nervous and erratic; it broke across sense and hurried always onward; it was self-consciously anti-literary and humble—working-class, it might be fair to say." Justice's preference for the parsing line is obvious here—as obvious as J. V. Cunningham's disdain for it. But preference is not the point. While I have for strategic purposes examined poems that highlight different kinds of lines egregiously (end-stopped, parsing, annotating), the point is that most free verse cannot afford to confine itself to any one of these procedures. As "The Snow Man" demonstrates, the drama, the purpose, the thrill of a free verse prosody lies in the ability to shape the speed and movement of a poem through the strategic use of different kinds of line endings. Line determines our experience of a poem's temporal unfolding. Its control of intonation creates the expectation for meaningfulness, an expectation that thrills because it might be as easily thwarted as fulfilled. When the different kinds of line endings I've examined are used in consort with one another, then all line endings become a means of annotating syntax.

How horrible it is, says Frank Bidart in his long poem "The Second Hour of the Night" to come to "the end of the line" and discover that every person we have ever desired is

the same, the same, the same, the same, the same

—which is a pentameter line on the model of Shakespeare's "Never, never, never, never, never." Bidart is describing an emotional predicament, but he wants us to feel an aesthetic challenge buried within it. We need a highly nuanced line to keep our poems from standing still, and, more than that, we need a line capable of many different effects, one that will save us from mere repetition of the same effect, however compelling it might be.

In one sense, "The Second Hour of the Night" is about Myrrha, mother of Adonis and daughter of Cinyras, for whom Myrrha develops an incestuous passion. Ovid tells the story in the *Metamorphoses,* and, in Bidart's hands, the story becomes an allegory for fate: when she finally sleeps with her father, Myrrha "enters" a realm that she already "contains." But if the subject matter of Bidart's poem is harrowingly explicit, the poem also seems like an allegory of its own formal procedures. Like Myrrha, the poem's maker must enter, be entered, enforce acts of entering. Listen to the poem's culminating passage, which is a single sentence stretched across twenty-one lines.

On such a night, at such an hour,

when the inhabitants of the temple of
delight assume for each of us one
profile, different of course for each of us,

but for each of us, single:—

when the present avatar of powers not present though
present through him, different for each of us,

steps to the end of the line of other, earlier
inhabitants of the temple of
delight, different for each of us:—

when the gathering turns for its portrait

and by a sudden trick of alignment and light and
night, all I see

the same, the same, the same, the same, the same—

on such a night,

at such an hour

> . . . grace is the dream, half-
> dream, half-
>
> light, when you appear and do not answer the question
>
> that I have asked you, but courteously
> ask (because you are dead) if you can briefly
>
> borrow, inhabit my body.

This sentence is about what happens at the end of the line. Before he introduces the subject of the sentence (delayed until the sixteenth line), Bidart interweaves three different kinds of line ending, orchestrating intonation, speed, and our expectation for lexical and syntactical repetition. Preceding the independent clause ("grace is") are three adverbial clauses, each placed at the beginning of a line at the beginning of a stanza: "when the inhabitants"; "when the present avatar"; "when the gathering." As in the first half of "The Snow Man," these line endings organize the syntax, highlighting its repetitions. But within each clause the lines are either heavily enjambed ("temple of / delight") or end-stopped ("different of course for each of us, // but for each of us, single"). The enjambments push us through the syntax, consistently throwing emphasis on the beginning of the line: "each of us one / profile"; "not present though / present"; "line of other, earlier / inhabitants." Then the end-stopped lines lock us in place, each of these lines concluding with the same phrase: "different for each of us." Along the way, stanza divisions occur only after end-stopped lines.

But just when this pattern of annotating the syntax seems to become dependable, the third adverbial clause disrupts the pattern. Here, syntax extends for only one line before a stanza division intrudes, parsing the syntax ("turns for its portrait // and by"). Then, instead of culminating with the phrase "different for each of us," the syntax arcs across another stanza division and introduces something different from "different": "the same, the same, the same, the same, the same." Finally, as if to confirm the suspicion that we've gotten precisely nowhere, the opening line of the sentence reappears, this time broken in half: *"on such a night, / at such an hour."* The phrase *"on such a night"* is also the opening line of the entire poem. We have come to the end of the line.

Or have we? "Within repetition," Bidart says elsewhere in "The Second Hour of the Night," "is the moment when each step / backward is a step / downward, when what you move toward moves toward // you." The passage I've been examining is a dramatization of this wish, for just when everyone we've ever loved has turned out to be the same person, the syntax, enjambed thrillingly across both stanza and line, erupts in something different ("all I see // the same, the same, the same, the same, the same"). In this sense, the repetition of the poem's opening line signals that we have gotten somewhere indeed: we've come to the subject of the sentence, "grace"—a vision of the dead lover who returns to animate us, to make us different from ourselves, to tell us that we are doomed to repeat neither a past with no future nor a syntactical pattern with no predication. Having confronted the end of the line, we discover that just when the line appears to end most definitively—a pentameter consisting of the repetition of the same two syllables five times—the syntax continues. And it continues with a rush, offering us the poem's most radically enjambed lines so far: "grace is the dream, half- / dream, half- // light, when you appear." This moment is the culmination of the entire poem, the moment at which the special case of Myrrha's suffering is redeemed in the mirror of common human experience.

"It is the end of the line," wrote Randall Jarrell in 1942, speaking not of lines as such but of the poetry of Pound, Eliot, Williams, Stevens, and Moore: "Today, for the poet, there is an embarrassment of choices: young poets can choose—do choose—to write anything from surrealism to imitations of Robert Bridges." That field of choice had by 1942 been open for a long time—at least since Pound and Eliot began writing rhymed quatrains; but polemical attachment to one kind of line or another has occluded the field. Hence the value of "The Second Hour of the Night," a poem that doesn't make us choose between different kinds of lines but rather forces us to recognize the implications of formal decisions poets make with every line they commit to paper.

To cast syntax into lines is to provide choices, to place precision in the service of equivocation by making us consider the implications of reading the syntax in one way rather than another. So if line determines the way a sentence becomes meaningful to us in a poem, it also makes us aware of how artfully a sentence may resist itself, courting the opposite of what it says—or, more typically, something just slightly different from what it says. Writing free verse is not, as Frost once quipped, like playing tennis with the net down; it is like playing tennis on a court in which the net is in motion at the same time that the ball is in motion. But to have said so is to have discovered the limitation of the metaphor: whenever we come to the end of the line, no matter how we've gotten there, the net is never standing still.

III. *Forms of Disjunction*

THINK OF THE FINAL LINES of great poems. "Drink and be whole again beyond confusion." "I have wasted my life." Think of the way in which the poem brings us to that line.

> Row, row, row your boat
> Gently down the stream—
> Merrily, merrily, merrily, merrily
> Life is but a dream.

A quatrain in ballad meter: alternating lines of tetrameter and trimeter. The first line veers toward spondees, the second establishes the trochaic lilt, the third breaks out in a string of dactyls, and the fourth line returns us to the lilt but with a difference. The thrill of that line lies in its unpredictability. We row our boat, row it again. We're working, but the stream flows gently; so do we, the work of rowing merged with the sound of water flowing. And suddenly—who could have known that our work and our pleasure would come to this?—life is but a dream: the power of these words, no matter how familiar, emanates not so much from the words themselves as from the leap that has taken place between the third and final lines of the poem. It is the same kind of leap that distinguishes the end of James Wright's "Lying in a Hammock at William Duffy's Farm in Pine Island, Minnesota"—

> In a field of sunlight between two pines,
> The droppings of last year's horses
> Blaze up into golden stones.

I lean back, as the evening darkens and comes on.
A chicken hawk floats over, looking for home.
I have wasted my life.

—or the end of Robert Frost's "Directive": "(I stole a goblet from the children's playhouse.) / Here are your waters and your watering place. / Drink and be whole again beyond confusion."

We often associate disjunction—the leap from one semantic, discursive, or figurative plane to another—with modernism; we think of Rimbaud, of Ezra Pound. We often associate an even more aggressive mode of disjunction with postmodernism; we think of Ashbery, of Charles Bernstein. But disjunction has always been a crucial aspect of poetry. The thrill of the final two lines of "Western Wind," one of the oldest poems in the English language, can be described in much the same way that I've analyzed "Row, row, row your boat."

Western wind, when will thou blow,
    The small rain down can rain?
Christ, if my love were in my arms
    And I in my bed again!

The expostulation—Christ!—marks the place where the poem breaks open, releasing an emotion that is both unpredictable and, at least in retrospect, logical. The poem could not be otherwise, yet it surprises us, and the surprise is permanent. How well Yeats knew this to be true; he ended his life's work with a calculatedly unassuming poem called "Politics."

And maybe what they say is true
Of war and war's alarms,
But O that I were young again
And held her in my arms.

How then did certain modern poets (Eliot more than Yeats, Pound more than Eliot) purchase this quality for themselves, lulling us into the illusion that Frost's web of syntax and meaning is placidly discursive? A completely satisfying answer to this question would need to serve many different constituencies, both aesthetic and social. But each of those constituencies would need to begin by noticing that even within a very circumscribed notion of modernism disjunction takes different forms and has different effects. Here is the opening passage of "The First Sermon," the central movement of *The Waste Land.*

> The river's tent is broken: the last fingers of leaf
> Clutch and sink into the wet bank. The wind
> Crosses the brown land, unheard. The nymphs are departed.
> Sweet Thames, run softly, till I end my song.
> The river bears no empty bottles, sandwich papers,
> Silk handkerchiefs, cardboard boxes, cigarette ends
> Or other testimony of summer nights. The nymphs are departed.
> And their friends, the loitering heirs of city directors;
> Departed, have left no addresses.
> By the waters of Leman I sat down and wept . . .
> Sweet Thames, run softly till I end my song,
> Sweet Thames, run softly, for I speak not loud or long.
> But at my back in a cold blast I hear
> The rattle of the bones, and chuckle spread from ear to ear.
> A rat crept softly through the vegetation
> Dragging its slimy belly on the bank
> While I was fishing in the dull canal
> On a winter evening round behind the gashouse
> Musing upon the king my brother's wreck
> And on the king my father's death before him.
> White bodies naked on the low damp ground
> And bones cast in a little low dry garret,
> Rattled by the rat's foot only, year to year.
> But at my back from time to time I hear
> The sound of horns and motors, which shall bring
> Sweeney to Mrs. Porter in the spring.
> O the moon shone bright on Mrs. Porter
> And on her daughter
> They wash their feet in soda water
> *Et O ces voix d'enfants, chantant dans la coupole*!

The passage begins with what appears to be naturalistic description: the river, its banks. Still, we pay more attention to what is missing (bottles, sandwich papers, cigarette ends, nymphs, city directors) than to what is there. And at the same time, the logic of naturalistic description has begun to crumble, since the absence of sandwich papers has been equated with the absence of nymphs. The landscape seems simultaneously rural and urban, arcadian and modern, and the intrusion of the lovely refrain from Spenser's "Prothalamion" ("Sweet Thames, run softly, till I end my song") does not seem merely ironic; rather, it makes us wonder if there is some unknown presence in this desiccated landscape, an undiscovered power in the verse to perceive it. The subsequent quotation from Marvell (itself disrupted by "The rattle of the bones, and chuckle spread from ear to ear" instead of the expected "Time's winged chariot hurrying near") builds our sense of an uncanny presence to an almost unbearable pitch. The lines do not seem merely willful or irrational; rather, they are all the more frightening for appearing to suggest a hidden logic we have yet to fathom. By the second reference to Marvell, Eliot's disjunctions run rampant, sweeping us from the rat's foot to motor cars to Mrs. Porter and finally to the inexplicable epiphany of Verlaine's children chanting in the dome.

We don't stay there. Eliot's manipulation of the grail myth at least partially unites these disjunctive voices, and once we know that the line from Verlaine's sonnet describes Parsifal's arrival at the grail castle, the poem's logic seems clearer. But our knowledge does little to reduce the poem's thrilling effect. Eliot's disjunctions take us to different places at the same time, and we're left feeling that we occupy different registers of consciousness at the same moment. Even more crucially, Eliot's disjunctions are the result of eccentric, overlapping voices. When the voice of "Prufrock" suddenly stops its gentle whining to intone "In the room the women come and go / Talking of Michelangelo"—or when the tired voice of "Gerontion" startles us with "In depraved May, dogwood and chestnut, flowering Judas, / To be eaten, to be divided, to be drunk / Among whispers"— we have the sense of some logic other than the speaker's personality determining the direction of the lines. The effect is as if we'd seen a ghost, or heard one. It is the feeling, writ large, that we have at the end of "Western Wind" or "Row, row, row your boat": *life is but a dream.*

In contrast, consider the opening lines of the second canto of Pound's long poem.

Hang it all, Robert Browning,
there can be but the one "Sordello."
But Sordello, and my Sordello?
Lo sordels si fo di Mantovana.
So-shu churned in the sea.
Seal sports in the spray-whited circles of cliff-wash,
Sleek head, daughter of Lir,
         eyes of Picasso
Under the black fur-hood, lithe daughter of Ocean.

This poem contains, as does every poem Pound wrote, lines of exquisite beauty—"Seal sports in the spray-whited circles of cliff-wash": long, image-freighted lines that now sound more like Charles Wright than Pound himself. But Pound's ideogrammatic method doesn't necessarily produce the uncanny power that Eliot's disjunctions do. In Eliot there is always the shock produced by shifting from one mode of logic or discourse or image to another; in Pound the method is usually pedagogical rather than dramatic, a momentary puzzling over what *Sordello* might have to do with So-shu churning in the sea.

Let's call Eliot's mode *wet* and Pound's *dry*. Think of more contemporary examples: Jorie Graham is wet, her disjunctions as dramatic as Eliot's, as potently charged with anxiety, loss, rage, fear.

I will vanish, others will come here, what is that,
never to lose the sensation of suddenly being
completed in the wind—the first note of our quarrel—
it was this night I believe or possibly the next
filled with the sensation of being suddenly completed,
I will vanish, others will come here, what is that now
floating in the air before us with stars a test case
that I saw clearly the impossibility of staying

I'm not yet concerned with what these concluding lines of "Le Manteau de Pascal" mean. I want to register the way in which this compressed, disjunctive syntax evokes not so much a speaker as a rivetingly engaged act of speaking. Consider in contrast Rosmarie Waldrop's use of dry disjunction in *A Key into the Language of America*.

here
the wind
will be tomorrow
a constant disquisition
into the secret of
velocity
while men grow small
within their skin
tongue tied
into another language

Waldrop offers a stern rejection of the bardic aspect of poetry, which Graham sometimes courts. Equally attractive is her refusal to idealize her own stylistic choices; she once began writing collage poems in order to stop writing about her mother, discovering that the collage poems were also about her mother. But unlike Graham or Eliot, Waldrop is interested in language but not in the drama of speaking—as if our sense of the illusion of the unified speaking subject demanded that we no longer act as if we entertain that illusion productively. Human feeling is staved off by a disjunctive style that stakes its authority on the constructedness of human feeling.

The allure of dry disjunction often depends on the impression that the poetry is performing serious work by disrupting normative discursive patterns; a didactic imperative overrides the distraction of pleasure. But if dry disjunction may sometimes run the risk of seeming schoolmasterish, it may at other times sound like the bad boy in the back of the classroom: the didactic imperative becomes a joke that hinges, as does most complex irony, on the hope that somebody else won't get it. John Ashbery mastered this mode of disjunction early on, and he occasionally returns to it in more recent poems such as "Notes from the Air."

A yak is a prehistoric cabbage; of that, at least, we may be sure.
But tell us, sages of the solarium, why is that light
still hidden back there, among the house-plants and rubber sponges?

This aspect of Ashbery's achievement has been extremely influential, but what distinguishes him from his imitators is the fact that Ashbery is a master of both wet and dry disjunction. Not only does he move between these modes from poem to poem; he moves between these modes within a single poem, building a highly nuanced drama of diction and sensibility. As "Notes from the Air" continues, it reprimands itself: "No more trivia, please." Then the poem concludes with a burst of lyrical beauty that sounds like the most Wordsworthian passages in Stevens.

> No more trivia, please, but music
> in all the spheres leading up to where the master
> wants to talk to you, place his mouth over yours,
> withdraw that human fishhook from the crystalline flesh
>
> where it was melting, give you back your clothes, penknife,
> twine. And where shall we go when we leave? What tree is bigger
> than night that surrounds us, is full of more things,
> fewer paths for the eyes and fingers of frost for the mind,
>
> fruits halved for our despairing instruction, winds
> to suck us up? If only the boiler hadn't exploded one
> could summon them, icicles out of the rain, chairs enough
> for everyone to be seated in time for the lesson to begin.

People who complain that all of Ashbery's poems are pretty much about the same thing (loss, longing, the passage of time) need to admit that all lyric poems are pretty much about the same thing. Ashbery refuses to disguise this uniformity; he forces us to recognize that we read a poem for its manner rather than its matter. And once we pay attention to the manner, we feel the impact of his virtuoso manipulations of disjunction. "Notes from the Air" is an extremely moving poem. Dear God, it says, give me back my childhood, my penknife, my twine. As I die, let me remember that no world I've ever imagined, no world beyond, could possibly be more beautiful than the world I've lost—these trees, this sky.

How does Ashbery get away with this? By encasing these feelings in a highly nuanced sequence of different modes of disjunction. More precisely, the poem's sense of possibility, loss, and recovery is registered in these shifts between modes. Or to put it another way, the disjunctiveness of "Notes from the Air" is dramatic. Ashbery's range of diction is wider than Eliot's, but like Eliot's or Graham's, his poems feel spoken even if they lack an easily identified speaker: their disjunctive manner does not preclude the fiction of the human subject, however intricately constructed the manner might suggest the fiction to be. Rather than relying on heavily fragmented syntax, consequently, Ashbery's disjunctiveness depends on the collision of normative syntax and wayward argument; the poems sound as if they ought to make logical sense but never quite do. As a result, the poems are always ripe with pathos. The extremely wet "Note from the Air" concludes by reintroducing a hint of dry disjunction ("If only the boiler hadn't exploded"), as if to say that we need to return to trivia in order to entertain the poem's delicate emotions.

John Koethe, a poet both heavily influenced by Ashbery and immediately distinguishable from him, pushes this method even farther. By restricting himself almost exclusively to wet disjunction, he risks an astonishing continuity of tone, and the tone is often startlingly sentimental; it is indebted as much or more to late Jarrell than to Ashbery.

> I feel like someone living in a fable
> Of his own construction, waiting in some bleak, completely
> Isolated country with no hope or history, where the minutes
> Come and go and memories displace each other, leaving nothing
> For the soul to do but feel them as they flow, and flow away.

These lines from "The Constructor" describe simultaneously a state of mind and the movement of the poem. The moments slide past us, taking everything with them: all disparity, all surprise is embraced by an endlessly unfolding syntax. "I want to feel things burst again," says Koethe, and to entertain the illusion that there is "something more," the poem itself must burst. Just when Koethe admits that all he can do is construct "long, erotic sentences expressing / An unfocused state of sadness," something unpredictable happens.

> There was this chorus of strange vapors, with a name
> Something like mine, and someone trying to get free.
> You start to see things almost mythically, in tropes
> And figurations taken from the languages of art—to
> See your soul as sliding out of chaos, changeable,
> Twice blessed with vagueness and a heart, the feelings

Cumbersome and unrefined, the mood a truly human one
Of absolute bewilderment; and floating up from that
To an inanimate sublime, as though some angel said
Come with me, and you woke into a featureless and
Foolish paradise your life had gradually become.

This passage is the climax of a poem that seems to dismantle the possibility of climax. Koethe retains the placid, determined syntax (there is no illusion here of breaking out of normative structure) but the shift in diction and argument is breathtaking—all the more breathtaking because the syntax helps to occlude the fact that with the phrase "chorus of strange vapors" we have entered a new linguistic realm. If Koethe is certain that all we can do is live in a fable of our own construction, he is also certain that this realization gets us nowhere. It does not prevent us from being swept up in illusions. It does not prevent us from requiring the unpredictable beauty of disjunction—the wish that something might disrupt the endless continuity of our lives. The soul sliding out of chaos. A mood of absolute bewilderment. An angel whispering *Come with me.* Who would have thought that "The Constructor," one of the most relentlessly disillusioned poems ever written, could conclude by finding solace in such beautiful, time-honored nonsense?

Every sentence is a kind of experiment. We begin a sentence not knowing where or how it will end. We release it to the world unable to predict the response it will, fairly or unfairly, elicit. The sentences in a poem are obviously premeditated in ways that our speech can never be. But great sentences in great poems feel as shocking as the sentence that, once uttered, elicits the laughter or the derision we never expected. Some sentences display their astonishment more obviously than others. Derek Walcott: "At the end of this sentence, rain will begin." Who could have known? Charles Wright: "A turkey buzzard logs on to the late evening sky." Gertrude Stein: "A sentence is this." Wordsworth:

Ye powers of earth, ye genii of the springs,
And ye that have your voices in the clouds,
And ye that are familiars of the lakes
And of the standing pools, I may not think
A vulgar hope was yours when ye employed

Such ministry—when ye through many a year
Thus, by the agency of boyish sports,
On caves and trees, upon the wood and hills,
Impressed upon all forms the characters
Of danger or desire, and thus did make
The surface of the universal earth
With meanings of delight, of hope and fear,
Work like a sea.

Everything about this sentence—the parataxis, the rolling pentameters, the proliferation of abstract nouns—is working to prepare us for the jump to figurative language in the last four words: "Work like a sea." Most simply, this figure itself works to blend the feelings denoted by those abstract nouns: hope with fear, hope and fear together with delight. But the effect of the figure is unpredictably disruptive. Beginning with an inverted foot (a trochee rather than the expected iamb), the figure pulls us into a different landscape, both literally and metaphorically. In lines immediately preceding those I've just quoted, Wordsworth describes how stopping short on ice skates once provided the illusion that the world wheeled past him—a sense that the world was animated by inexplicable powers. Wordsworth then addresses the powers he himself has imagined ("Ye powers of earth, ye genii of the springs") and with the final simile ("Work like a sea") returns us to the ordinary world that prompted the illusion. More uncanny than the address to unseen powers is that final simile: it lifts us to another world but also returns us to a world we've never left behind. *Life is but a dream.*

One could paraphrase the final line of "Row, row, row your boat" this way: *poetry is disjunctive.* Wordsworth and Ashbery. "Western Wind" and Jorie Graham. A poem unempowered by disjunction would seem as intolerable as a life without change, discovery, or defiance. It would seem content with what it knows. Once wet disjunction has been differentiated from dry, once we see that powerfully disjunctive movement takes place within (not in spite of) normative syntax, then we are free to feel the shock of Wordsworth or Frost as liberally as we feel the shock of Eliot or Ashbery.

With this freedom comes risk. When W. H. Auden wrote the introduction for Ashbery's first book, *Some Trees,* he rightly placed Ashbery in line with Rimbaud. In order to be true to the nature of "subjective life," said Auden, these poets "must accept strange jux-tapositions of imagery, singular associations of ideas." The danger, as Auden admitted more openly in a letter to Frank O'Hara, was that of "confusing authentic non-logical relations which arouse wonder with accidental ones which arouse mere surprise and in the end fatigue." Auden sounds sure of himself, but how is an "authentic" form of nonlogical relation to be distinguished from an "accidental" one?

There is always a risk involved in disjunction; that's part of its wonder. And we need to feel, in our pleasure, the threat of the accident impinging slightly on the authentic. Listen, finally, to the end of Charles Wright's "Stray Paragraphs in April, Year of the Rat."

> If we were to walk for a hundred years, we could never take
> One step toward heaven—
> 	you have to wait to be gathered.
>
> Two cardinals, two blood clots,
> Cast loose in the cold, invisible arteries of the air.
> If they ever stop, the sky will stop.
>
> Affliction's a gift, Simone Weil thought—
> The world becomes more abundant in severest light.
>
> April, old courtesan, high-styler of months, dampen our mouths.
>
> The dense moist and cold and dark come together here.
>
> The soul is air, and it maintains us.

Wright builds this poem from two- and three-line stanzas that are always syntactically closed but that may be broken internally. What determines the order of these stanzas? Each seems so discrete that its connections to other stanzas becomes increasingly tenuous as the poem moves forward. Finally, in the last stanza, Wright separates the three lines from each other—as if the principal of disjunction that determined the movement from stanza to stanza has now invaded the space of the stanza itself: each line feels like its own metaphorical universe. And in the same way that Wordsworth's simile erupts at the end of the sentence, Wright's strategically improbable metaphors introduce moments of thrilling disjunction within the lines.

Yet the poem feels like anything but a collection of stray paragraphs. Consider those final three lines. A line of fifteen syllables is followed by one of twelve, then one of nine; or, to put it another way, a line of eight stresses is followed by one of five, then one of three. That first line veers toward spondees but feels generally dactylic: "old courtesan"; "high-styler of"; "months, dampen our." The second line begins by extending that spondaic pattern ("dense moist") but then becomes more placidly iambic. So at the same time that the lines are diminishing in length, they are also growing quieter, slower: "The soul is air, and it maintains us." In addition, the three lines are bound together by an intricate pattern of sonic echo—consonants (*months, mouths, moist*) and vowels (*old, cold, soul*). The poem's nonlogical relations feel authentic because the tone of the poem, conveyed through its music, is so palpably clear. We trust the poem because it wants to be listened to, spoken, savored in the mouth before it is understood. The sound invites us into the poem, making us feel that we will be listened to in return.

I said earlier, apropos of the distinction between Eliot and Pound, that dry disjunction tends to work by precluding the lure of human feeling: it also tends to distrust lyric pleasure. I don't mean to draw inviolable distinctions here; Charles Wright has learned as much or more from Pound as he has from Stevens. But to do so, Wright had to separate the schoolmasterish Pound from the poet who could not often enough admit that he himself was seduced by the beauty of language. We row our boat, row it again. We're working, but the stream flows gently; so do we, the work of rowing merged with the sound of water flowing.

IV. *Song and Story*

THE AUDIENCE IS ASSEMBLED, the introduction delivered, and the poet walks to the podium. "Just a few things first," says Charles Bernstein in a poem called "Poem."

> let's see
> a dog, well for those of you not
> from here—a rather common domestic
> pet, four legs, tail.
> I should say
> the seasons in the poem refer
> to the seasons in the northeast
> so that fall refers to the leaves
> falling and winter is cold and usually
> gray—often
> I will use the seasons
> in a metaphoric way,
> as you will see.

Anyone who has ever attended a poetry reading will get this joke by around the third line, but Bernstein pushes through hilarity to an issue close to any poet's heart: the real life of a poem inheres in how it sounds. If the first allegiance of "Poem" is to what it says, then the pure music of Bernstein's "Johnny Cake Hollow" would seem to offer a welcome alternative.

> Xo quwollen smacked unt myrry flooped
> Sardone to fligrunt's swirm, ort

Jirmy plaight org garvey swait ib
Giben durrs urk klurpf.

The audience grows restless. Bernstein offers a translation of "Johnny Cake Hollow" ("Ceylon's ox slaked Mary's gourd / Cycloned to flagrant dawn, sat / Jimmy's plight on gravy sprain as / Gibes in fairies lorn"), but its familiar words don't necessarily offer common sense. "Poem" and "Johnny Cake Hollow" are both strategic exaggerations of ordinary poetic strategies, and together they make the same point: a poem that stakes its claim exclusively on sound will only travel so far as a poem of *what* and *why*.

If "Poem" is all story and "Johnny Cake Hollow" is all song, most of Bernstein's poems dwell in a middle ground where the semantic power of language is alternately bolstered and resisted by the physical seduction of its sound—a place where we are given the freedom to take pleasure in language that we may not need fully to understand. This is the place where all poems dwell, some more flagrantly than others.

> We twa hae run about the braes,
>   And pou'd the gowans fine;
> But we've wandere'd mony a weary fitt,
>   Sin auld lang syne.

Braes: riverbanks. Gowans: daisies. Paving the way for the later Romantic poets, Robert Burns reinvigorated the lyric not simply by turning to Scots but by allowing his readers to take pleasure in the sound of words without necessarily worrying about their sense.

Bernstein wants to reawaken us to that shock, and his poems embody the notion that we feel the tactile pleasure of language to the degree that our misunderstandings are not easily elided. It might be tempting to say that Bernstein engages in an arduous struggle with signification, but "misery loves euphony" is his true mantra. So while he occasionally writes lines of quiet lyric beauty, he is ultimately seduced by dissonance, lines in which the music of language moves the narrative in ways we couldn't have expected.

The glue uncorked smelled sweeter than
a carriage ride through heaven but turned many
an head in opposite confection.

The direction of this story turns on confection—on the poet's manipulation of the tension between the sonic and semantic aspects of language. The poem does not retreat to the angelic ideals of pure sound or transparent meaning but revels in their resistance of each other.

American literary culture has long been marked by the dream of separating a poetry of sheer linguistic play from a poetry weighed down by subject matter, but in fact our most compelling poets have always thrived on the inevitable tension between these aspects of language. Writing in the 1931 Objectivist issue of *Poetry* magazine, Louis Zukofsky distinguished "sincerity" (language "which records action and existence") from "objectification" (language "which is an object" in itself). By the latter phrase Zukofsky did not mean that words refer unambiguously to objects but that language becomes an object of our attention once we focus on its aural properties. Neither did Zukofsky wish to oppose objectification to sincerity: although the former is recognized as the "satisfaction derived from melody in a poem," it is achieved through "the arrangement, into one apprehended unit, of minor units of sincerity." Poetry written in the Objectivist tradition may be known more for its song than its story, but Zukofsky was adamant that poets could not possibly be free to sacrifice one of these properties of language to the other.

Consider this early version of George Oppen's "Debt," called "The Manufactured Part." The poem tilts toward the pole of sincerity: we are told a story.

So let us speak, and with some pride, of other men.
Not passengers; the crew.

Or the machine shop. For the planet
Isn't habitable but by labor—

We are alone and live by labor—
Benches, and the men,
The noise, the shock

Of the press where for an instant on the steel bed,
The manufactured part!

New.
Newly made. Imperfect, for they made it; not as perfect
As the die they made which was imperfect. Checked
By some mechanic. What percent
Of human history, so little said of it.

The final version of "Debt," published in *The Materials,* Oppen's
second volume of poems, tilts toward the pole of objectification
or song.

That 'part
Of consciousness
That works':

A virtue, then, a skill
Of benches and the shock

Of the press where an instant on the steel bed
The manufactured part—

New!
And imperfect. Not as perfect
As the die they made
Which was imperfect. Checked

To tolerance

Among the pin ups, notices, conversion charts,
And skills, so little said of it.

The Objectivist movement in poetry was not about focusing language on objects but about the achievement of form. Both versions of "Debt" feel like George Oppen; they both have something
to say about work he experienced as both a laborer and a labor
organizer. But the final version feels more quintessentially like Oppen because the focus on a physical act also feels like the explo-
ration of a metaphysical problem. How does Oppen enact this transformation?

Most obviously, Oppen discards the opening expositional lines of the earlier version, lines that establish a clear, if provisional, sense of the poem's speaker and subject matter: "So let us speak, and with some pride, of other men." More crucially, the final version of "Debt" moves forward not so much by the unfolding of its story as by the exquisitely calibrated turns of its lineation. In the first version, the syntactical movement from the line "The noise, the shock" to the line "Of the press where for an instant on the steel bed" feels like a narrative movement, the acquisition of information. In the final version, the three lines beginning with the word "of" make us more aware of the syntax as syntax. It's not just that we wonder for a moment what "a skill / Of benches" or "the shock // Of the press where an instant" (rather than "the shock / Of the press where *for* an instant") might mean; we feel the movement from a slow, stress-packed line ("A virtue, then, a skill") to a more rapid line ("Of benches and the shock") to a line not only longer but more generously larded with unstressed syllables ("Of the press where an instant on the steel bed") until finally the syntax lands on a monosyllable that feels like the manufactured part itself: "New!" The first version of "Debt" is about manufacturing, and so is the second version; the narrative content of the two poems is pretty much the same. But in the second version we are encouraged to hear the language of the poem at work: something has been made.

Oppen was one of the twentieth century's most dazzling makers of lines. Reading him, it is impossible not to be aware of how, in the strategic absence of meter and rhyme, line becomes the crucial means by which a poet controls stress, intonation, and speed. But if Oppen is a poet whose first allegiance is to sound, he is also a poet of sincerity, in Zukofsky's sense of the word. Twenty-five years passed between the publication of *Discrete Series* and *The Materials*: Oppen had nothing to say. More precisely, he had no pressing work that a poem could perform effectively. During those years from 1934 to 1962, Oppen joined the Communist Party, organized the Farmers' Union milk strike, made patterns for Grumman Aircraft, landed in Marseilles with the 103rd Antitank Division, received a Purple Heart, moved to Mexico to avoid being called before the House Un-American Activities Committee, built houses, made furniture, and, as his unaffected correspondence reveals, devoted himself to raising his daughter. "There are situations which cannot honorably be met by art," said Oppen. "Some ideas are not politically useful, or useful to the childhood of a daughter."

Many other poets might be scrupulous enough to recognize that the usefulness of poetry depends on a frank appraisal of its limitations; few but Oppen would raise familial responsibility along with the more obviously prestigious call of social responsibility. Art wasn't worth anything to Oppen unless it honored places and people around him, and neither was art worth much unless it honored its own appetite for form. His respect for the act of making, no matter how small, is at every moment palpable, and it infuses his work with a sweetness that makes difficulty feel like life's reward. Through language we may experience the world intimately, says Oppen, but we will never understand it, encompass it, exhaust it. "That they are there!" exclaims Oppen in "Psalm" when he sees wild deer bedding down in the forest.

> Their eyes
> Effortless, the soft lips
> Nuzzle and the alien small teeth
> Tear the grass.
>
> The roots of it
> Dangle from their mouths
> Scattering earth in the strange woods.
> They who are there.
>
> Their paths
> Nibbled thru the fields, the leaves that shade them
> Hang in the distances
> Of sun
>
> The small nouns
> Crying faith
> In this in which the wild deer
> Startle, and stare out.

At moments like this, Oppen aspires to a poetry of sheer being, a poetry in which the wonder is not the self but the fact that there is something for us to stand on. Respect for the world and appetite for form are merged in such a poetry: "this in which" the world stares back at us is the poem itself.

This in Which is the title of Oppen's third book of poems, published in 1965. He would go on to publish four more volumes of poetry, but for some readers, Oppen would remain the poet of *Discrete Series,* the slender book of 1934 that inaugurated both his career and his silence. Ron Silliman, who was associated with Bernstein's magazine *L=A=N=G=U=A=G=E* in the 1970s, once regretted that Oppen's later work placed increasing importance on what the poem "says," thereby transforming "the aesthetically radical and oppositional poetry of the early thirties to a more conservative (aesthetically, if not politically) phenomenon which then served as the foundation for the ensuing middle road." Oppen's leftist politics are not in question here, but neither is the prestige of what American literary culture has learned to recognize as aesthetic extremity. If Oppen's political values are equally as compatible with a poem that "says" something as with a poem that "is" something, what then is truly at stake in Oppen's turn toward poems like "Psalm"? What are we saying if we say that a poem places too much importance on the story it tells?

Think back to the two versions of Oppen's "Debt." If the second version seems to place less importance on what it says, it is because Oppen alters the poem's syntax and lineation. Lines explaining that the manufactured part is "imperfect, for they made it; not as perfect / As the die they made which was imperfect" do not provide more information than lines explaining that the part is "imperfect. Not as perfect / As the die they made / Which was imperfect." The latter lines feel more reticent, however, because the syntax has been reduced to fragments ("imperfect") or because otherwise unaltered syntax has been broken into lines that emphasize rhythmical units rather than complete semantic units ("As the die they made" rather than "As the die they made which was imperfect"). Similarly, to explain that the part is "Checked // To tolerance" rather than "Checked / By some mechanic" is to make the poem seem more impersonal, lacking in the presence of the human subject we associate with having something to say.

At stake here is not so much the content of the poem as the attitude taken toward it. The second version of "Debt" may feel more impersonal, but in general Oppen became increasingly less shy about displaying human feeling as his career moved forward; in "Psalm" even the deer are charged with human presence. So inasmuch as most poetry written in the Objectivist tradition avoids openly emotional subject matter, it might be said that Oppen's later work challenges aesthetic expectations rather than paving the middle road. More instructive is the simple recognition that Oppen's poems demonstrate the inseparability of story and song, sincerity and objectification, aural pleasure and experimental form. He is in this regard as radical a poet as Robert Burns or Charles Bernstein.

"It is a mistake," says Bernstein in his verse essay "The Artifice of Absorption," to think of "formally active poems as / eschewing content or meaning." With the word "artifice" Bernstein gestures toward the visceral pleasure of a poem's language: objectification. With the word "absorption" he acknowledges a poem's capacity to make us disregard its language, allowing us to concentrate instead on what the poem says: sincerity. "Anti-absorptive" writing distracts us from what is said, forcing us to pay attention to the sonic qualities of the language—to the "rhetoricity" of the language rather than "the / rhet- / orical / effect."

> The re-
> di-
> rection
> of at-
> ten-
> tion-
> al
> focus
> can
> as use-
> ful-
> ly be
> located
> in the
> shift
> of at-
> tention
> from the
> rhet-
> orical

effect
(the thing
said/de-
picted)
to the
rhetoricity.

Like "Poem" and "Johnny Cake Hollow," this sentence represents
an exaggeration of an ordinary poetic strategy: turning against not
only the syntax but the syllables, these lines make us experience the
temporal unfolding of the poem's language in one particular way and
not in another. But as the sentence demonstrates, egregious artifice
does not prevent us from being absorbed in what the poem says: we
land on the unbroken five-syllable word "rhetoricity" and absorb its
meaning securely. So while "The Artifice of Absorption" does not
go so far as to embrace openly emotional subject matter, it is fueled
by a powerfully coherent argument at the same time that its lineation
disrupts the usual decorum of argument, begging us to pay attention
to how the language sounds. The very phrase "Artifice of Absorption" is designed to remind us that artifice and absorption cannot be
mutually exclusive categories. Only by artifice are we absorbed; only
by confection do we discover direction.

If it is a mistake to think of formally active poems as eschewing
content or meaning, it is also a mistake to think of story-telling poems
as eschewing highly artificial formal strategies. Here is a story.

> Four hands, three legs and half
> a brain, my uncle said: what my grandmother
> salvaged from the war—her brother's wounded sons,
> sullen Ed with his limp, Grover hunched and simpering.
> They worked the fields and in the barn, ate in her kitchen,
> hair slick from washing up, like the hired hands.

Here is a song.

> Four hands, three legs and half
> a brain, my uncle said: what my grandmother
> salvaged from the war—her brother's wounded sons,
> sullen Ed with his limp, Grover hunched and simpering.

They worked the fields and in the barn, ate in her kitchen,
hair slick from washing up, like the hired hands.
When she said grace,

my grandmother said it standing,
bandaging her hand in her apron skirt
to lift the cast iron skillet out of its round hole
to the square table of men. Burn herself up, her daughters said,
on Sundays, visiting like me, and scolding my uncle,
but still she fed with her fingers the squat stove,
and her grown wards

chopped the wood and hauled it,
pumped water, hauled it, cut hay, hauled it, hauled
the pig and cow and chicken shit and stirred the flies.
You keep out of the barn, my uncle said, after he'd found me
rapt by what they'd found: thick braid hung from a beam—
two blacksnakes writhing there like a hot wire,
a lit fuse.

What else do you need to know?

These stanzas from Ellen Bryant Voigt's "Art of Distance" comprise
seven iambic lines: a trimeter followed by a pentameter, a hexameter,
a heptameter, another hexameter, another pentameter, and a final
dimeter. We feel the spondaic force of "a lit fuse," a dimeter line
with two stressed syllables side by side, because it sounds different
from the more consistently iambic "When she said grace." We feel
the density of "pumped water, hauled it, cut hay, hauled it, hauled"
because this mostly monosyllabic pentameter encourages us to place
an extra stress on "hay," a syllable that should remain unstressed, as
it does in the more (but not exclusively) iambic "bandaging her hand
in her apron skirt." We feel another spondaic thrust at the end of "but
still she fed with her fingers the squat stove" because the intrusion of
extra unstressed syllables ("with her fingers the") speeds up the line
before the collision of stressed syllables ("squat stove"), a collision
made more forceful both by the longer duration of the vowels in
"squat stove" and by the line's strategically artificial syntax (not "she
fed the squat stove with her fingers" but "she fed with her fingers the
squat stove"). This is a poetry whose first allegiance is to music, a

poem whose stature as a thing made out of words it is impossible to underestimate.

But after five sentences stretched over three stanzas, a syntactically complete line intrudes—"What else do you need to know?" This intricate dance of pattern and variation is stuffed with narrative information. Overstuffed: Ed and Grover, to whom the grandmother is an aunt; the unnamed uncle who is the grandmother's only son, brother to her daughters; the one daughter who is herself the mother of the child who can take her eyes off neither the blacksnakes coupling in the barn nor the stump of her second cousin's (that would be Ed's) amputated leg: "I looked at it hard." In this story, we depend on song to carry us forward even when we know so much we couldn't possibly know what else we need to know. Despite its glut of narrative information, "The Art of Distance" is nothing like Bernstein's "Poem," which is funny because it treats the question "what else do you need to know?" as an uncomplicated question.

Voigt is one of our most emotionally forthright poets because she is also one of our most formally active poets. She would agree with Bernstein that no good poem allows words to become transparent, "replaced by / that which they depict, their 'meaning.'" But if she seems more interested in the confluence of song and story than in their dissonance, her mission is nonetheless to honor the misperceived, the partially understood. "Wrinkle coming toward me in the grass—no," begins "The Art of Distance," dramatizing the necessarily error-ridden process of recording experience. If all things were alike, if meaning were always perspicuous, then poetry's endlessly variable negotiation of story and song would be superfluous. If all things were different, if a story could never be told, then the allure of sound would be lost. There would be no meeting place, no place of resistance. Error would be uninteresting rather than provocative.

"I am not exactly aware," said Mr. Micawber after a rousing chorus of "Auld Lang Syne," "what gowans may be, but I have no doubt that Copperfield and myself would frequently have taken a pull at them, if it had been feasible." By satirizing the pleasure we take in sounds we do not necessarily understand, the author of *David Copperfield* was reminding us that even when we read exclusively for story we never want to know the whole story, every *what* and *why* converted reliably into *this* and *because*. We enjoy semantic coherence when it feels sufficiently at risk. We thrill to the likeness of sounds because aural coherence does not guarantee that our desire to know the whole story will be fulfilled.

> We twa hae paidl'd in the burn,
> > Frae morning sun till dine;
> But seas between us braid hae roar'd,
> > Sin auld lang syne.

Burn: water. Braid: broad. Poetry sets us on the broad sea, and we're pulled forward by incantation, drawn back to what resists our intelligence almost successfully.

V. *Untidy Activity*

"WHAT ONE SEEMS TO WANT in art, in experiencing it," said Elizabeth Bishop, "is the same thing that is necessary for its creation, a self-forgetful, perfectly useless concentration." This sentence makes the hard work of art seem simultaneously rare and available to everyone. It suggests that the making of works of art is a way of being alive. Uselessness has been a distinguishing feature of a work of art since Kant, but anyone who dreams or falls in love has known the feeling Bishop identifies: a freedom to forget ourselves so that we might discover we are different from ourselves.

How does the act of a poem, the act embodied in its being written or being read, instill this feeling in us? How can poetic language simultaneously ask us to imagine a world and incite us to forget it, distracting us from it simultaneously renders viscerally *there?*

> The frowsy sponge boats keep coming in
> with the obliging air of retrievers,
> bristling with jackstraw gaffs and hooks
> and decorated with bobbles of sponges.
> There is a fence of chicken wire along the dock
> where, glinting like little plowshares,
> the blue-gray shark tails are hung up to dry
> for the Chinese-restaurant trade.
> Some of the little white boats are still piled up
> against each other, or lie on their sides, stove in,
> and not yet salvaged, if they ever will be, from the last bad storm,
> like torn-open, unanswered letters.

The bight is littered with old correspondences.
Click. Click. Goes the dredge,
and brings up a dripping jawful of marl.
All the untidy activity continues,
awful but cheerful.

Here, at the end of "The Bight," Bishop faces the loss of possibility. She surveys the water at low tide; it is sheer but reveals nothing of interest. Pelicans crash into the water with unnecessary fervor ("like pickaxes"), surfacing with nothing to show for their efforts. The dredge goes click, click. Yet the feeling evoked by this scene is not merely awful because the poem's language is forever slipping into new connotations. Bishop alerts us to the possibility of transformation by suggesting that the clicking of the dredge sounds like "perfectly off-beat claves." The boats return obligingly, like retrievers; shark-tails glint like plowshares. And although one can even smell the brackish water "turning to gas," one "could probably hear it turning to marimba music" if "one were Baudelaire."

The subject of "The Bight" is poetic language—more precisely, the power of figurative language to provoke in us a feeling of self-forgetfulness. We are invited to picture the "little white boats" piled up like "torn-open, unanswered letters," and the bight is "littered with old correspondences" both figuratively and literally: figuratively in the sense that only boats, not letters or retrievers or plowshares, are present; literally in the sense that, as Baudelaire put it in "Corre-spondences," our world is made up of nothing but figures—"forests of symbols" in which any given word brings to mind another word. The "untidy activity" to which Bishop refers at the end of "The Bight" is both the action of the dredge and the action of the poem's language, which has not only presented a vividly precise scene but also allowed the precision to ramify, encouraging us to forget that scene (claves, letters, Baudelaire). The poem renders a landscape of loss in a language of possibility.

Bishop embraces Baudelaire, but the notion of correspondences was sometimes treated suspiciously by twentieth-century poets who wanted their words to cling single-mindedly to objects. "Le Paradis n'est pas artificiel," wrote Ezra Pound in the *Pisan Cantos,* turning on Baudelaire's *Les Paradis Artificiels* and then on W. B. Yeats.

> Le Paradis n'est pas artificiel
> and Uncle William dawdling around Notre Dame
> in search of whatever
>
>   paused to admire the symbol
> with Notre Dame standing inside it
> Whereas in St Etienne
>   or why not Dei Miracoli:
> mermaids, that carving.

Pound objects to the notion of correspondences because he wants to be liberated from associations that have accumulated around a particular thing. Rather than the all too meaningful cathedral of Notre Dame, he prefers the pristine beauty of Pietro Lombardo's tiny stone mermaids in the church of Santa Maria dei Miracoli in Venice. He wants poets to employ a kind of diction that would emphasize the thing referred to rather than the exfoliating connotations of the word.

But even if Baudelaire's symbolist inheritors oversimplified the notion of correspondences, Baudelaire himself was no more interested in predictable meanings than Pound was. The world is alive, says Baudelaire in Richard Howard's translation, with "perplexing messages": one object conjures the obscure memory of another, one word slips precariously to the next, and our attention is drawn as much by the vagaries of sound as of sense. Proust's notion of involuntary memory depended crucially on Baudelaire's example, and Proust at every moment emphasizes the vagaries of the mnemonic process. To look at one thing is to think of another thing; to utter one word is inevitably to be distracted by its relationship to other words—to enter the space of untidy activity.

From this perspective, Baudelaire's notion of correspondences is not a way of predicting how the universe fits together, but a way of acknowledging that the effect of the words we use is always to a degree out of our control. The language of a poem inevitably encourages us to forget what we are simultaneously compelled to remember, and poets who want to emphasize the iconic relationship of words and things are giving the strategic impression that their words do not participate in an uncontrollable network of associations. The opposition between Baudelaire and Pound, between symbolism and objectivism, between a poetry that forgets what it points to and a poetry that merely points, depends less on how language actually functions than on what poets say about their language, either by manifesto or by dramatizing the work of language as a thematic element in a poem.

Consider this little poem by William Carlos Williams: "El Hombre."

> It's a strange courage
> you give me, ancient star:
>
> Shine alone in the sunrise
> toward which you lend no part!

Like Pound, Williams praises an object for standing alone, for being nothing but itself, and he wants to foster the impression that his words work in the same way, denoting only their objects and rejecting any extraneous correspondences. "One obvious characteristic of a literary text," says Richard Poirier, "is that its words tend to destabilize one another and to fall into conflicted or contradictory relationships. Some writers, like Shakespeare, happily indulge in this situation and profit from it, while others . . . are insufficiently alert to the resulting pressures that build up in a work." Is Williams insufficiently alert or is his little poem a dramatization of what it means to suppress correspondences?

In "Nuances of a Theme by Williams," Williams's friend Wallace Stevens quotes "El Hombre" and adds two variations.

I

> Shine alone, shine nakedly, shine like bronze,
> that reflects neither my face nor any inner part
> of my being, shine like fire, that mirrors nothing.

II

> Lend no part to any humanity that suffuses
> you in its own light.
> Be not chimera of morning,
> Half-man, half-star.
> Be not an intelligence,

Like a widow's bird
Or an old horse.

Stevens's fanciness may seem at odds with Williams's plainness, but
in fact Stevens is playing out the implications of Williams's poem,
not turning against it. "Shine alone in the sunrise," says Williams
to the morning star, making it stand paradoxically for something
other than itself: it becomes a figure for the poem's aesthetic. "Shine
alone," repeats Stevens. "Shine nakedly," he continues, emphasizing
the morning star's singularity but also extending its figurative power:
the morning star is not only like a poem but like a human body.
"Shine like bronze, / that reflects neither my face nor any inner part
/ of my being," he adds, continuing to describe the morning star's
independence in language that cannot help but to remind us of its
place in chain of metaphorical correspondences. By the time we
reach its final lines ("Be not an intelligence, / Like a widow's bird /
Or an old horse"), the poem has pushed this paradox to the point of
hilarity. We have forgotten utterly the object that the poem wanted to
impress on our memories. The playfulness of the poem feels serious:
it suggests that we may delight in the untidy activity of language rather
than suppressing it.

Nothing can be forgotten if it has not first been remembered,
however, and we need to feel the specter of tidiness haunting the ongoing process of open-ended forgetfulness; in "The Bight" Bishop
is careful to say "untidy activity" rather than "messy activity," just as
elsewhere she says "uninteresting" rather than "dull," "unbeliever"
rather than "skeptic," and "un-rediscovered" rather than "lost forever." She is reminding us that even the most beautifully open-ended
poem is strategically so. But while the writing of a poem is mostly
painstaking work, the act of reading or writing feels at some point
like surrender to a state of mind beyond our capacity to will. As if for
no reason, an image makes us feel simultaneously at home and at sea:
at home because the image has seemed to choose us, at sea because
although we crave this feeling we cannot explain why we have been
chosen. A poem will be written if in the grip of memory we are able to
forget—if we are able to hear the brackish water of the bight turning
into marimba music.

Imagine wanting something to dream about. What object will be
strong enough to become an emblem of your desire? Why will you

ignore thousands of objects, hundreds of people, in order to fix on one? Imagine wanting to write a poem. You might see a red bird lying by the side of the road. Or an apple tree. It makes you think of the tree that grew in the yard when we were children. Standing beside it, a woman in a yellow dress. She leads you to the edge of the water where other children are playing. Across the lake, there is a party. Grownups moving as if asleep.

> He leaned forward over the paper
> and for a long time saw nothing.
> Then, slowly, the lake opened
> like a white eye
> and he was a child
> playing with his cousins,
> and there was a lawn
> and a row of trees
> that went to the water.
> It was a warm afternoon in August
> and there was a party
> about to begin.

These are the opening lines of Mark Strand's "The Untelling," the final poem in *The Story of Our Lives*. The lines tell a story about beginning, and the wish of the poem is never to end: the poem's protagonist has found himself in the grip of memory, and in order to move forward he needs to forget. Recalling Bishop's preference for words that conjure their ghostly opposites, he must "untell" rather than "rescind." Only by untelling can the story be told.

Enacting this process, "The Untelling" alternates between free verse passages describing its protagonist and blank verse passages in which the protagonist rewrites the memory. In these untellings, the child is terrified by the prospect that nothing will change: watching the grownups, *"it seemed as if nothing would enter / their lives to make them change, not even the man / running over the lawn, waving a sheet / of paper and shouting."* But with each untelling, this scene grows increasingly ominous because of the threat of change. The urgency of the man running over the lawn suggests that something may have happened without our knowing it—something horrible— but further attempts at discovering why only intensify the mystery.

As detail accumulates in each new account of the memory, contradictions appear. Contrary associations disrupt the story's teleology, and the more we seem to have remembered, the more we feel haunted by the associations of everything we have forgotten. Eventually, the protagonist writes with the growing awareness that he himself will be forgotten.

> *Already the full moon*
> *had risen and dropped its white ashes on the lake.*
> *And the woman and the others slowly began*
> *to take off their clothes, and the mild rushes of wind*
> *rinsed their skin, their pale bodies shone*
> *briefly among the shadows until they lay*
> *on the damp grass. And the children had all gone.*
> *And that was all. And even then I felt*
> *nothing. I knew that I would never see*
> *the woman in the yellow dress again,*
> *and that the scene by the lake would not be repeated.*

In these lines, a poem that began as a recovery of childhood has been transformed into a vision of the impending mortality of both the child and the mother—"*the one in the yellow dress whose name / I had begun to forget.*" Darkness is descending. And the desperate man has always arrived too late: "he would never catch up / with his past."

This realization is more cheerful than awful. In "a creative and spontaneous being," says D. W. Winnicott, one finds "a capacity for the use of symbols," by which he means figurative language in general. Children spend most of their time in a psychic space that is neither completely internal nor completely objective—the "potential space" of play. Adults may too readily capitulate either to a world of inanimate objects or to a world of uncontested fantasy, but the healthy adult continues to live in increasingly complex and tenuous versions of potential space. Language becomes a place where we live. And because we don't necessarily expect a poem to be useful in obvious or immediate ways, the language of poetry is liberated to create this potential space, hovering between the literal and the figurative.

Their pale bodies shone
briefly among the shadows until they lay
on the damp grass.

This scene could be taking place outside the window or across the Lethe, river of forgetfulness; it feels at once earth-bound and otherworldly. So while Strand's protagonist knows for certain that he *"would never see / the woman in the yellow dress again,"* the poem nonetheless repeats these simple words again and again (*woman, yellow, lake*), transforming the recognition of permanent loss into a vision of infinite variability. Experience and the loss of experience are often difficult to distinguish in great lyric poems, and "The Untelling" dramatizes the process that most poems perform implicitly: it creates an event (the poem itself) that carries us beyond the story of loss the poem set out to tell.

Strand uses language in a way that Baudelaire, Stevens, and Bishop would recognize: while his diction is everywhere precise, he embraces a word's propensity to conjure other words, allowing us to experience the feeling of self-forgetfulness as a gift rather than a lapse from other responsibilities. Poets who have tried to curtail this propensity might respond that those responsibilities are urgent: certain events must not be forgotten, some stories must never be untold. In the foreword to her *Collected Early Poems*, for instance, Adrienne Rich chastises the young poet who wrote "Storm Warnings," the first poem in her first book: "Nothing in the scene of this poem suggests that it was written in the early days of the Cold War, within a twenty year old's earshot of World War II, at the end of the decade of the Warsaw Ghetto and Auschwitz, Hiroshima and Nagasaki, in a climate of public fatalism about World War III."

But it isn't exactly true to say that nothing in the poem "suggests" the impingement of these public events on the private act of writing. What Rich means is that instead of naming events directly, the language of "Storm Warnings" creates an aura of associations. For while none of the historical cataclysms of the twentieth century are named in the poem, the poem does register an awareness of these events through its figurative language; W. H. Auden was able to speak confidently of "the historical apprehension expressed in 'Storm Warnings.'" But for the later Rich, the kind of precision idealized by Pound and Williams is preferable to the kind exemplified by Stevens or Strand. Her sense of the deficiencies of "Storm Warnings" culminates in a list of events, and increasingly, her own poems have taken the form of lists.

> Catch if you can your country's moment, begin
> where any calendar's ripped-off: Appomattox
> Wounded Knee, Los Alamos, Selma, the last airlift from Saigon.

Compare these lines from Rich's "Atlas of the Difficult World" to a passage from "Seven Poems within a Matrix for War," Michael Palmer's sequence of poems concerning the Gulf War of 1991. Palmer is a poet associated more with Pound and Williams than with Stevens and Strand, yet he approaches historical events through the highly equivocal language of correspondences.

> In the hole we found beside the road
> something would eventually go
>
> Names we saw spelled backward there
>
> In the sand we found a tablet
>
> In the hole caused by bombs
> which are smart we might find a hand
>
> It is the writing hand
> hand which dreams the hole
>
> to the left and the right of each hand
>
> The hand is called day-inside-night
> because of the colored fragments which it holds
>
> We never say the word desert
> nor does the sand pass through the fingers
>
> of this hand we forget
> is ours

These lines are marked by a civilian's experience of the war: the sequence employs the military jargon of the late twentieth century ("smart bombs," "desert storm"), and part of the sequence is dated, reminding us of its location in a particular moment. Yet the historically specific language of the poem does not feel sundered from the possibility of new and unpredictable associations; in fact, Palmer's language feels as liminal as Strand's: "hole," "sand," "road," "desert." The language invokes a specific place at a specific time but also conjures other landscapes, ghostly worlds. And rather than suggesting that history exists independently of the mind recording it, the poem suggests that over time the past exists for us as what Winnicott called potential space. "From the screen poured / images toward me. // The images effected a hole," says Palmer in the beginning of the sequence: he is describing the overwhelming way in which the Gulf War pervaded the media, and his poem embodies the notion that by employing the language of the war we continue to write it with a "hand we forget / is ours." The story is untold in the telling.

Memory, says Palmer, recalling Bishop and Strand, is a kind of "unlistening." And it is through this activity that responsibilities are honored, not in spite of it: Palmer's poems invite us to question their assertions, participating in the ongoing task of formulating and reformulating the history of our time. Given that language is always meaning one thing because it threatens to mean another, this self-interrogation is ultimately unavoidable. But for some poets, the fact that the words "hole" and "hand" do not point inevitably to one location would be problematic. For Palmer, this duplicity is not in itself remarkable: it is simply the way language functions in the world, and he delights in it, making it crucial to our experience of the poem.

So while Palmer is known as a poet who has absorbed poststructuralist notions of language, the language of his poetry is not eccentric. "What if things really did / correspond, silk to breath // evening to eyelid / thread to thread," he asks in his "Baudelaire Series," implying that if correspondences were predictable we would be left with nothing to think about, no means of thinking: a thread would be a thread. "Words say, Misspell and misspell your name," insists Palmer in honor of Baudelaire, "Words say, Leave this life." This poetry embraces untidy correspondences because they are the inevitable work of language itself.

"All language," said Emerson, high priest of forgetfulness, "is vehicular and transitive, and is good, as ferries and horses are, for conveyance, not as farms and houses are, for homestead." This is true, he explained, because "every sensuous fact" is ridden not only with double or quadruple meaning but with "much more manifold meaning": our attempt to curtail these exfoliating connotations is gloriously doomed to failure. Still, as much as we may revere the feeling of self-forgetfulness, the feeling cannot be willed. Sometimes we are immune to a word's unceasing allure; at other times we may feel it deeply but fail to articulate it in poems that are inevitably driven by will—by a self-determination that may threaten to foreclose the very openness on which self-forgetfulness depends.

This is why Baudelaire needs throughout *Les Fleurs du Mal* to dramatize not only the joyous eruption of correspondences but also the moribund inability to be possessed by vehicular language. This is why Bishop longs to be forgotten as easily as the world forgets itself. And this is why Stevens is not simply correcting his friend's misconception about language in "Nuances of a Theme by Williams," spinning variations on Williams's invocation of the sun. Stevens is entering an inevitable dialectic in which the power of a word's untidy activity depends on our inability to recognize it dependably, in which the power of self-forgetfulness is contingent on the specter of self-loathing—the inability ever to forget ourselves. To deny a metaphor's ability to distract us from what it also says is to place ourselves at odds with the pleasure of poetry. But if the language of poetry were not haunted by failure, by its inability to distract us, we could never forget it.

VI.   *The Spokenness of Poetry*

WHAT DO WE WANT when we want a poem to have a voice? Two hundred years after the appearance of *Lyrical Ballads,* Louise Glück published *The Wild Iris,* a book of talking plants. "I tell you I could speak again," insists the iris: "whatever / returns from oblivion returns / to find a voice." Every flower has something urgent to say, but throughout *The Wild Iris* the act of speaking disperses the presence of a speaking subject. To speak is to be shattered; to treasure the illusion of an unmistakable voice is to be next to nothing. A poet who writes poems in the voices of poppies and violets is not simply choosing to disguise herself in order to reveal herself; she is asking us to reconsider the force a metaphor with which we have grown comfortable. Flowers don't really have voices.

A number of modern poets made highly influential remarks about the dramatic nature of lyric utterance. "Everything written is as good as it is dramatic," said Robert Frost. "In the search for 'sincere self-expression,'" said Ezra Pound, "one gropes, one finds some seeming verity," casting off "complete masks of the self in each poem." In the middle of the twentieth century, the New Critical synthesis of these remarks transformed a means into a method, and by the time Cleanth Brooks and Robert Penn Warren published *Understanding Poetry,* it could be taken for granted that all poetry involves a dramatic organization. The method leads us to prefer modern poems that announce themselves immediately as voice driven ("That is no country for old men") and encourages us to look back to older poems that prefigure the preference ("For Godsake hold your tongue, and let me love").

As this continuity between the twentieth-century Yeats and the seventeenth-century Donne suggests, the New Critical preference for the dramatic poem helped to perpetuate the illusion that the nineteenth century had been a bad time for poetry—the gradual attenuation of Wordsworth's bold decision to place the poet at the center of the poem. But in fact the modern notion of the persona is a refinement of a crucial turn in Victorian poetics. There are two extremes toward which any particular poet might lean, explained Robert Browning in his 1852 essay on Shelley: the "subjective" poet "whose study has been himself" and the "objective" poet "whose endeavor has been to reproduce things external." While Browning had begun his career as a highly subjective poet, he moved quickly toward the opposite pole, writing the dramatic monologues for which he remains best known. Tennyson's career followed a similar trajectory. A dramatic poetry offered these poets the best of two worlds: the seduction of an inner self at work and the suggestion that the poet's self remained occluded.

But if all poems are in some sense dramatic, uttered by a speaker who is not necessarily the poet, how should the dramatic monologue be distinguished from any lyric poem? Many of the New Critics were troubled by this question, and in retrospect it doesn't seem coincidental that the first good taxonomy of the dramatic monologue was formulated at the same moment that the prejudice against the Victorians was beginning to be dispelled. Stressing the continuities between Tennyson and Eliot, Robert Langbaum suggested in *The Poetry of Experience* that in a dramatic monologue we feel a strategic tension between our need to judge the speaker and our desire to sympathize with the speaker. Reading Tennyson's "Ulysses," for instance, we are free to entertain a longing for oblivion because we feel a disparity between what Ulysses says and what he understands.

> The lights begin to twinkle from the rocks:
> The long day wanes: the slow moon climbs: the deep
> Moans round with many voices. Come, my friends,
> 'Tis not too late to seek a newer world.
> Push off, and sitting well in order smite
> The sounding furrows; for my purpose holds
> To sail beyond the sunset, and the baths
> Of all the western stars, until I die.
> It may be that the gulfs will wash us down:

> It may be we shall touch the Happy Isles,
> And see the great Achilles, whom we knew.

Ulysses wants to die before he dies, to sail beyond the sunset before the sun sets. The wish is paradoxical, but because Ulysses seems unaware of the contradiction, his utterance seems not merely paradoxical but poignant. "We have lingered in the chambers of the sea / By sea-girls wreathed with seaweed red and brown / Till human voices wake us, and we drown," says T. S. Eliot's Prufrock, who owes to Ulysses not only the languidness of his tone but the mechanism of his dramatic utterance as well. Reading "The Love Song of J. Alfred Prufrock," we feel again the poignancy of the speaker's wish because we also recognize the lack of self-understanding that fuels it. We are allowed to entertain the wish to be submerged, to be forgotten, and simultaneously encouraged to step away from it.

Robert Langbaum's point was that these poems are ironic: we know where the speaker stands, and we feel that the poet is not necessarily asking us to stand with him. But if this logic will elucidate many poems we think of as dramatic monologues, it will not account for all of them. Both "Ulysses" and "Prufrock" conclude with a wish to dissipate the self in a larger element—as if their voices could survive only by being dispersed. What if a poem began with that wish rather than ending with it? Listen to Hart Crane's "Repose of Rivers."

> The willows carried a slow sound,
> A sarabande the wind mowed on the mead.
> I could never remember
> That seething, steady leveling of the marshes
> Till age had brought me to the sea.
>
> Flags, weeds. And remembrance of steep alcoves
> Where cypresses shared the noon's
> Tyranny; they drew me into hades almost.

This river knows what it feels like to have a surface and a depth; it knows the terror of standing revealed in broad daylight, and it knows the hidden forces of the unconscious. Like Ulysses, it feels the allure of hell. And if it were ever tempted by tranquility, seduced by the "singing willow rim" of a pond, it also knows that tranquility must be earned: emotion recollected in tranquility, Wordsworth's definition of poetry, is this river's true repose.

> And finally, in that memory all things nurse;
> After the city that I finally passed
> With scalding unguents spread and smoking darts
> The monsoon cut across the delta
> At gulf gates . . . There, beyond the dykes
>
> I heard wind flaking sapphire, like this summer,
> And willows could not hold more steady sound.

Reading "Repose of Rivers" as well as "Ulysses," we understand that the poet has adopted an egregiously artificial voice, one that cannot be taken simply for his own. But while Tennyson encourages us to believe in the fiction of his speaker, Crane does not ask to forget the artifice: rivers don't read Wordsworth. Nor do we simply feel a tension between what the water says and what it understands about its journey to the sea. On the one hand, we read "Repose of Rivers" as the story of a young man's entry into sexuality; forces initially threatening to the self (scalding unguents, smoking darts) become forces that ultimately consolidate the self. On the other hand, we read "Repose of Rivers" as the story of a river's progress from marsh to gorge to pond to city to sea. Reading the poem, we know we are swimming in two streams at once, as it were, and it is their simultaneity rather than their ironic tension that intrigues us. The self implied by the poem's utterance is consolidated inasmuch as it is also divided.

"You should know," says the multiminded clover to the apparently single-minded poet in *The Wild Iris*, "that when you swagger among us / I hear two voices." This is almost always the case, no matter if we conceive of a lyric poem as an essentially dramatic utterance, no matter if we think of the dramatic monologue as essentially different from the lyric. "It is terrible to survive / as consciousness / buried in the dark earth," says Glück's wild iris.

> You who do not remember
> passage from the other world
> I tell you I could speak again: whatever

returns from oblivion returns
to find a voice:

from the center of my life came
a great fountain, deep blue
shadows on azure seawater.

These lines ask us to imagine a dormant tuber wakened by a little
spring rain. Simultaneously, they express a poet's darkest dilemma:
the knowledge that the act of once having written a poem in no way
guarantees the realization of another poem. But if it is not completely
satisfying to say that the poem is spoken by a perennial plant, neither
is it satisfying to say that the poem is spoken by a poet. For if the
final lines strike us as a splendid metaphor for the relief of breaking
into song after long silence, they also strike us an accurate account of
the plant's sudden eruption into flower. The jump to a third level of
figuration (the emerging flower and voice are like "a great fountain,
deep blue / shadows on azure seawater") does not subsume the
fictions of poet and plant but rather triangulates them with a third
element. To find a voice in *The Wild Iris* is to discover the interplay
of voices: the dormant self disperses itself in the act of speaking. "Not
I, you idiot, not self," say the scilla, "but we, we—waves / of sky blue
like / a critique of heaven."
 Heaven itself speaks in *The Wild Iris*.

When I made you, I loved you.
Now I pity you.

I gave you all you needed:
bed of earth, blanket of blue air—

As I get further away from you
I see you more clearly.
Your souls should have been immense by now,
not what they are,
small talking things.

These lines from "Retreating Wind" allow us to postulate a voice for
heaven only inasmuch as we also hear other voices: a gardener talking
to her plants, a mother talking to her children, and a poet talking to her

poems—poems that are themselves "small talking things." Nowhere does Glück allow us the unmitigated pleasure of losing ourselves in the fiction of a coherent self anterior to language. "Go ahead: say what you're thinking. The garden / is not the real world." We know this to be the case; flowers don't have voices. But it takes a flower to remind us that poems don't really have voices either. "No one wants to hear / impressions of the natural world," say the daisies to the poet: "you will be / laughed at again; scorn will be piled on you."

Even if such moments of dialogue foster the impression of coherent speaking selves, the impression is strategically compromised by the fact that everybody in the book (flowers, poets, gardeners, parents, gods) speaks in pretty much the same register. As in Yeats's later plays, the voices are barely differentiated. But if these voices were not intended to be unique, neither may this tangle of voices be fused into a whole. To crave the uncompromised distinction of speakers is to crave a vision of perfect unity. And if *The Wild Iris* sometimes dangles these tempting extremes before us, its least resonant poems are those spoken most clearly by something we can imagine as an integrated subject; its richest poems neither disperse completely the sense that they are spoken nor cling resolutely to the fiction of an identifiable speaker. Reading them, we spend less time postulating a speaking subject and more time attending to the aural texture of the language, its spokenness. The dialogue within each poem takes precedence over the dialogue between them.

The Russian critic Mikhail Bakhtin called this kind of writing "dialogic," a linguistic tapestry woven from a wide variety of competing strands. Bakhtin was not talking about dialogue, an interchange between discrete voices that may reinforce the impression of their singularity; he was talking about the ways in which any utterance simultaneously promotes and dismantles the verbal embodiment of the self. These tensions are perceptible in a wide variety of texts, not only novels and poems. But so stubborn is the association of the lyric poem with the unified human subject that even Bakhtin could insist that a poet "is a poet insofar as he accepts the idea of a unitary and singular language and a unitary, monologically sealed-off utterance."

This is wrong not simply because it's possible to think of poetic performances that undermine the notion of a singular speaking voice more violently than Glück's, performances from Williams to Olson to Susan Howe. These poems ask us to confront the constructedness of a speaking voice in all lyric poetry, and, having read them, our more difficult challenge is to explain why poems that do not explode the speaking subject violently are nonetheless dialogical in their utterance: when a disruptive poetic gesture seems close enough to business-as-usual to be mistaken for it, we are forced to reconsider that business rather than positing an opposition to it. To one degree or another, no poem extends the illusion of an individual speaker without challenging that illusion; at the same time, no poem, no matter how strenuous its challenge, manages to avoid the illusion of being spoken.

This is true even of poems easily identified as dramatic mono-logues—poems that may run the risk of diverting our attention from what I am calling the spokenness of the language to the more easily graspable fiction of the self. It is not misleading to say that Browning's "Fra Lippo Lippi" is spoken by the early Renaissance painter, a monk who longs for and often participates in the sensuous life outside the cloister. But within the logic of the poem, Fra Lippo Lippi is locked within the fiction of his own voice, and he craves the dispersion of the self, the breakdown of the unified subject into a variety of competing utterances—what he calls "a sweep of lute-strings, laughs, and whifts of song."

> And I've been three weeks shut within my mew,
> A-painting for the great man, saints and saints
> And saints again. I could not paint all night—
> Ouf! I leaned out of window for fresh air.
> There came a hurry of feet and little feet,
> A sweep of lute-strings, laughs, and whifts of song,—
> *Flower o' the broom,*
> *Take away love, and our earth is a tomb!*
> *Flower o' the quince,*
> *I let Lisa go, and what good in life since?*
> *Flower o' the thyme*—and so on. Round they went.

In the final lines of this passage, the monologue is interrupted by a lyric extrusion, a song sung by a different voice, and these inter-ruptions continue throughout the poem, embodying Lippi's wish to be released from his cell—from the false restriction of being as-sociated with a single voice. Like the sea in Tennyson's "Ulysses," this poem moans round with many voices, as do all of Browning's greatest monologues. They are not necessarily interrupted literally, as "Fra Lippo Lippi" is, but they are at all times riddled with excess, an urge to dismantle the boundaries of the voice that the poems also erect. It is tempting to say that these monologues are exploded by a lyrical impulse—but not the lyric as Bakhtin would have understood it. "Lyricism," said the philosopher E. M. Cioran in a Nietzschean mood, "represents a dispersion of subjectivity. . . . To be lyrical means you cannot stay closed up inside yourself."

Glück has written monologues, but the closed self is for her, as for Lippo Lippi, a nightmare, and the need to resist its seduction is her great theme. Following *The Wild Iris,* she published *Meadowlands,* a book structured as a dialogue between discrete voices; subsequently, in *Vita Nova,* she wrote poems that mimic the dialogue between an analyst and analysand. It may seem that Glück is fracturing the self in these poems, but in fact these poems exteriorize as conflict what the poems of *The Wild Iris* suffer as ambiguity. In contrast, the richest poems of *Vita Nova* feel spoken inasmuch as each utterance contains a variety of overlapping, eccentric positions. These poems repeat themselves, hesitate, double back; they are more profoundly dialogical than the poems structured as dialogues.

In "Castile," for instance, Glück repeats and recombines a number of brief phrases: "orange blossoms," "children begging for coins," "I met my love," "the sound of a train," "I dreamed this." The poem begins by setting a scene.

> Orange blossoms blowing over Castile
> children begging for coins
> I met my love under an orange tree

Glück immediately questions this memory, wondering if the orange tree might have been an acacia tree, speculating that the memory might have been a dream. The poem begins again—and then again, telling and untelling the story it initially proposed.

> Castile: nuns walking in pairs through the dark garden.
> Outside the walls of the Holy Angels
> children begging for coins

When I woke I was crying,
has that no reality?

I met my love under an orange tree:
I have forgotten
only the facts, not the inference—
there were children somewhere, crying, begging for coins

Because each repetition of a phrase occurs in a slightly altered context, the multiple instances of the phrase feel both different and the same; the movement between them embodies the fluid, errant sense of memory that the poem describes. Near the end of "Castile" Glück remembers that she gave herself to her lover "completely and for all time," but the poem's commitment to movement undermines her assurance, confirming the vicissitudes of both poetry and love: "And the train returned us / first to Madrid / then to the Basque country."

This poetry exists in time. And to exist in time is necessarily to exist in repetition. And to exist successfully in repetition is to recognize that the past repeats itself always with a difference. Thematically, repetition allows memory to become a kind of forgetting, a release from the self; formally, it enables the poem to posit a future beyond the death of love. It is the mechanism by which Glück exists in the difficult middle, expressing the decentered, overdetermined nature of the self rather than seeking shelter in voice whose extremity is its distinctiveness. To posit a speaking self anterior to the language of the poem is to deny the temporal processes by which the self is constituted; it is to elide the problem, and the pleasure, of the poem's spokenness.

And yet we inevitably posit such speakers, just as we tend to believe in the simple integrity of the selves who sit across from us at breakfast. Such illusions are functional, even if they're driven by powerful wishes. For even if we have no particular reason to believe in the voices of flowers or rivers, who among us would not want to hear the voices of the dead?

don't worry   *I know you're dead*
but tonight

turn your face again
toward me

when I hear your voice there is now
no direction in which to turn

I sleep and wake and sleep and wake and sleep and wake and

but tonight
turn your face again

toward me

These opening lines of "The Yoke," by Frank Bidart, feel spoken, but they do not ask us to imagine a speaker distinguished by the particular nature of his speech: the lines repeat themselves in order to invoke different levels of consciousness or registers of speech, suggesting an interplay of voices within the dialogical texture of the poetry. The first line in roman type ("I sleep and wake and sleep and wake and sleep and wake and") plunges us into a life where repetition signals no possibility of change. In contrast, the preceding lines in italic type feel otherworldly; as Langdon Hammer suggests, they create "a space somehow interior to poetic discourse itself." In addition, the lines are themselves are about speech: they address a voice without a bodily source. But the lines also seem to describe our experience of reading these lines. We are encouraged to hear a voice, but we cannot locate it.

What's more, the lines seem conscious that we hear the voice of the dead—or the voice of a poem—because we fabricate that voice. When the opening lines are repeated in roman type, they feel suddenly urgent, repeated with a difference; the reorganization of the lines (the stanza break coming after "again" rather than "tonight") emphasizes the importance of turning "towards me." Then, like Fra Lippo Lippi gazing out the window of his cell, the poem erupts in the register of speech initially signaled by italic type.

see   upon my shoulders is the yoke
that is not a yoke

The yoke could be many things, perhaps the loss that makes imaginative compensation sweet. More important than identifying the yoke is registering the assertion-by-denial with which Bidart describes it: this poem asks us to imagine presences that are not present, voices that are not voices. We imagine we hear the poem's voices not because we can posit a face behind them but because we feel their interplay, one register of speech overlapping with another. The poem concludes by repeating its opening lines one more time. "Don't worry," we might say in response, "I know you're a poem." Like flowers and rivers, the dead don't really have voices.

What don't we want if we don't want to think of a poem as having a voice? We don't want to imply that human beings are undivided, fixed. We don't want to foster the impression that the poem occupies a timeless space, removed from the vicissitudes of experience, alien to the processes by which the self is constituted over time. But self-consciousness about the metaphorical status of a poem's speaker will not stop us from imagining the beautiful illusion of speech, just as a rational acceptance of mortality will not prevent us from craving the voices of the dead. The point is not necessarily to stop talking about a poem's speaker but to prevent that metaphor from disguising the intricate ways in which poems inhabit the problem of their spokenness. In any attempt to "communicate impassioned feelings," said Wordsworth in a note to one of the lyrical ballads, we find "a consciousness of the inadequateness of our own powers, or the deficiencies of language." That's what we want to hear.

VII.   *The Other Hand*

"TILL HUMAN VOICES WAKE US, " wrote T. S. Eliot in the final line of "The Love Song of J. Alfred Prufrock," "and we drown." What if Eliot had written,

> till other voices wake
> us or we drown.

George Oppen did write these lines: they are the final lines of the last poem in his last book. We do not necessarily feel doomed by our actions to drown; but neither do we feel that our actions have the power to save us from drowning. Does Oppen mean to suggest that we must choose between the act of waking to other voices and the act of drowning, or does he mean that these two actions are in some way interchangeable, that either action will to some degree substitute for the other?

In Latin, which had several different words for "or," the word *aut* was used to express an ultimatum: either X or Y. The words *sive* or *vel* were used to express a more equivocal set of alternatives: either X or Y but possibly both. Oppen specialized in the latter kind of "or," an "or" that presents a choice without necessarily forcing us to make it, an "or" that leaves us suspended between alternatives whose juxtaposition seems neither dismissible nor completely satisfactory. "What is or is true as / Happiness," says Oppen in "A Theological Definition," asking us to consider the ambiguous relationship of being and truth; the "or" blurs distinctions while at the same time asking us to consider what it would mean to make the alternatives more clearly distinct.

Oppen was not the only specialist in this kind of equivocation, of course.

> To be, or not to be, that is the question:
> Whether 'tis nobler in the mind to suffer
> The slings and arrows of outrageous fortune,
> Or to take arms against a sea of troubles
> And by opposing end them. To die—to sleep,
> No more; and by a sleep to say we end
> The heart-ache, and the thousand natural shocks
> That flesh is heir to.

In the first clause, Hamlet makes a distinction between being and not being, joins the two alternatives with an "or," and entertains the possibility of choosing between them. In the second clause the "or" reappears, suggesting that the alternatives of the second clause run parallel to those of the first clause: being is to suffering slings and arrows as not being is to taking arms against them. But the parallels seem provocative: in what way is choosing not to exist like taking arms? No "or" appears in the next clause ("To die— to sleep") but we wonder if one is implied: is the sense of this clause "to die *or* to sleep," suggesting that not being, taking arms, and dying are in some way equivalent (as opposed to being, suffering slings and arrows, and sleeping)? Or does the clause mean to say that dying and sleeping are equivalent to each other ("to die *is* to sleep")?

Hamlet's "or" perpetuates rather than closes down the discussion. In contrast, when Cleopatra says, "He shall have every day a several greeting / Or I'll unpeople Egypt," we feel the weight of the Latin *aut:* this "or" makes a distinction that demands to be observed. Likewise, when W. H. Auden says "We must love one another or die," we do not feel that we are being asked to think about the intricate relationship of loving and dying; after the line was altered to "We must love one another and die," the tension between the alternatives was lost. In what is not coincidentally the most famous rumination in English poetry, Hamlet's "or" makes distinctions only to make the choices between alternatives seem simultaneously more urgent and more difficult to make. The sound of this kind of "or" is the sound of thinking in poetry—not the sound of finished thought but the sound of a mind alive in the syntactical process of discovering what it might be thinking. "It must be visible or invisible, / Invisible or visible or both," said Wallace Stevens of the supreme fiction.

Jump forward to the twenty-first century.

> As when the flesh is shown
> to be remarkable
> most, for once, because
>
> markless:
> where the bruise
> was, that we called
>
> a bell, maybe, or
> —tipped,
> stemless—
>
> a wineglass, or just
> the wine spilling
> out,
>
> or a lesser lake viewed
> from a great height
> of air,
>
> instead the surprise that
> is blunder when it
> has lifted, leaving
>
> the skin to resemble
> something like clear
> tundra neither foot nor
>
> wing finds,
> —or shadow of.

In this, the first sentence of Carl Phillips's "Stagger," we are given a series of alternatives: four metaphors for the shape of a bruise (bell, wineglass, wine, lake) are connected by three "ors"; two metaphors for the skin after the bruise has healed (untouched tundra, un-shadowed tundra) are connected by a single "or"; and one of the metaphors for healed skin contains an additional "nor" (untouched by neither foot nor wing). These alternatives make the poem's momentum seem at once directed and dispersed. We do not feel called on to make a choice between the multiple metaphors, but we experience the process of deliberation between alternatives at once distant (bell and wineglass) and contiguous (wineglass and wine). We are lured into the poem's texture of partially overlapping choices, its stagger, and our satisfaction lies not in making a decision but in the equivocal process of understanding what the choices might be.

Phillips's poems are littered with "ors." Syntactically, "or" is his means of keeping the poem moving forward. In "The Pinnacle" he recalls playing a game in his head "called *Cross the Meadow // or Don't Cross It*" in order to push himself forward on a long walk: the poems do the same thing, deferring predication so that we will be drawn to the end of the poem. Thematically, "or" is the source of all spiritual possibility. Not to know choice is not to be human, to have no syntax. But to have made a choice is no longer to be fully alive, to come to the end of syntax. "Have I chosen / already," he asks in "The Clearing," "or is choice a thing / hovering yet"? Phillips's wish is to hover in the process of thought without a clear sense of teleology, and this wish feels rich because he questions its viability.

For like Hamlet, Phillips needs to worry that his finely developed taste for equivocation might become merely strategic, a way of holding the world at bay. But if there can be a romance to the infinite deferral of choosing, a romance of freedom, Phillips's "or" is not in service of the will. It is not a summoning of alternatives where none had existed; it is a recognition that because we exist in time, things become different from themselves. A turning face becomes a turned face. A bruise may seem at once like a bell or a wineglass or the spilled wine because it is difficult to account for the way in which the mark of injury passes, leaving us with no evidence that we were ever harmed. More damaging than the strategic deferral of choice is the romance of conviction—the assumption that we are free to be single-minded.

We want to be able to say "I experience the because," says Ludwig Wittgenstein in the *Philosophical Investigations*, emphasizing that single-mindedness depends on subordinating rather than coordinating conjunctions. We want, that is, to feel certain that one experience follows another for a reason, and we want to feel in charge of that forward motion. But if subordinating conjunctions make us feel more wayward than directed, not all subordinating conjunctions are alike. In a list of things connected by "and" rather than "or," our attention is directed more to the accumulation of things than to the act of accumulation.

> And the wind is still for a little
> And the dusk rolled
>   to one side a little
> And he was twelve at the time, Sigismundo,
> And no dues had been paid for three years,
> And his elder brother gone pious;
> And that year they fought in the streets,
> And that year he got out to Cesena
>   And brought back the levies,
> And that year he crossed by night over Foglia, and . . .

In these final lines from canto 8, Ezra Pound catalogs events from the life of the fifteenth-century condottiere Sigismundo Malatesta, leaving us to imagine a string of "ands" extending infinitely. Time is on Pound's mind, but we are not meant to wonder whether the year Malatesta crossed the Foglia to defeat a rival army came before or after the year he was attacked by a band of peasants in the streets of Rimini. The relentlessly paratactic syntax, highlighted by Pound's lineation, suppresses the passage of time, and we are left with the feeling that these events happen simultaneously—the sense, as Pound once put it, that all ages are contemporaneous. Without the subordinating conjunctions on which narrative movement depends, there is little sense of one event causing or producing or correcting another. Without the coordinating conjunction "or," there is little sense of a mind moving forward through the events, arranging them, wondering about them.

"Or" is the sign of a mind more interested in displaying a multiplicity of possible interpretations than in discerning something we could comfortably call the facts. At the same time, this mind is more palpably conscious of the pressure to call something a fact—to weigh one alternative against another before adding it to the available stockpile of information. Rather than feeling that all of history is contemporaneous, such a mind is possessed by a visceral awareness of the contemporary moment slipping forever away. Second by second, the incremental passage of time alters the sense of every preceding second, leaving this mind with a menu of more-or-less useful accounts. In addition, this mind is itself in motion, aware that one moment's version of events will not necessarily satisfy as time moves forward. Most important, this mind is not frustrated but nurtured by a constantly shifting sense of alternatives. "We remembered, we anticipated a peacock," says Proust of the continual process of surprise that constitutes our coming to know another human being, "and we find a peony."

The peony does not necessarily replace the peacock, canceling the earlier impression, but neither does it sit comfortably beside it. In a crucial passage in *Within a Budding Grove,* the second volume of *In Search of Lost Time,* Proust remembers seeing three trees at the entry to a covered driveway. Like the moment when he tastes the madeleine or feels the uneven paving stones beneath his feet, this moment instantly becomes overdetermined by associations he could never have predicted. Unlike those other moments, however, this glimpse of trees seems both powerfully meaningful and painfully obscure, and as Proust struggles to elucidate its claim on his attention, he explores the processes by which the madeleine or the paving stones come to feel so significant. The trees seem uncannily familiar; his mind wavers between past and present; the present loses its immediacy and shimmers with a sense of make-believe. Why? Had a similar vision lodged in his mind so long ago that he no longer remembered its origin? Or had he glimpsed the trees many years ago in a dream? One possibility generates another.

> Or were they merely an image freshly extracted from a dream of the night before, but already so worn, so faded that it seemed to me to come from somewhere far distant?

And another.

> Or had I indeed never seen them before, and did they conceal beneath their surface, like certain trees on tufts of grass that I had seen beside the Guermantes way, a meaning as obscure, as hard to grasp, as is a distant past, so that, whereas they were

inviting me to probe a new thought, I imagined that I had to identify an old memory?

And another.

Or again, were they concealing no hidden thought, and was it simply visual fatigue that made me see them double in time as one sometimes sees double in space?

The significance of the three trees might be due to a repressed memory or a distant dream or a recent dream or the essential mysteriousness of the trees themselves or the fatigue of the young man who glimpses them. "I could not tell," says Proust, who is left without the sudden memory of Venice provoked by the uneven paving stones or the childhood vistas conjured by the taste of the madeleine. Instead, he is left with the precarious mechanism on which those moments of recovery depend: the mind moving through a string of possibilities connected by "or."

This process is itself the reward of Proust's search, and he wants us to feel the slippage of time passing as much as Pound wants to suppress it. For Pound, the "factive personality" (as he called it) of Sigismundo Malatesta is made palpable through the accumulation of incidents connected by "and"; we build our sense of the personality by allowing those events to hover as it were simultaneously. For Proust, our sense of any human being is equally overdetermined, but he revels in the mind's capacity to grasp no more than a single impression at one time: he presents the mind's movement through alternatives rather than a stable concatenation of alternatives. As the young Marcel comes to know Albertine, for instance, he finds that she is many different people at different times, and, like Hamlet, he discovers in himself an equal variety of people. "I developed the habit," he remembers, "of becoming myself a different person, according to the particular Albertine to whom my thoughts had turned; a jealous, an indifferent, a voluptuous, a melancholy, a frenzied person." Considered abstractly, as a range of possibilities, these multiple selves exist contemporaneously, connected by "and"; experienced directly, as the visceral knowledge of a particular moment in time, these selves can be connected only by "or." One may be a peacock or a peony, an indifferent or a frenzied person, but not at the same second.

Proust's syntax is designed to embody this temporal movement. Among the sentences I've quoted from *Within a Budding Grove*, the most startling is the simplest—"I could not tell"—but only because this sentence is preceded by a long sequence of sentences in which predication is strategically delayed by apposition and subordination, forcing us to negotiate the plenitude of possibilities that make the simple sentence feel so resonant. Similarly, the most startling phrase in Carl Phillips's poem "Golden" is "two bodies, // fucking." But consider what happens next.

> two bodies
>
> fucking. It is difficult
> to see, but that much—
> from the way, with great
> then greater
> effort, their mouths
> seem half to recall or
> want to
>
> a song even older,
> holier than the one they
> fill with—I can
> guess.

These lines dramatize the process of a mind discovering that what it sees is the product of what it thinks. And thought, for Phillips as for Proust, is syntax. In the sentence I've just quoted, the subject of the second independent clause is delayed until the tenth line: "that much . . . I can / guess." In between, there is time for a thousand choices: "from the way . . . their mouths . . . recall . . . a song." What kind of song? A song "even older . . . than the one they fill with." Older in what sense? "Older, / holier." How do they recall the song? They recall it "with great . . . effort." Is their effort consistent? No, they recall "with great / then greater / effort." Is the effort successful? Perhaps—they "recall or / want to." Can we be certain that their physical gesture represents the mental act of recollection? No, "their mouths / seem half to recall." Emerging from this syntactical thicket, one sentence stretched over eleven lines, Phillips can "guess" with some certainty at what is otherwise difficult to see: "two bodies, // fucking." Phillips is not discouraged but enthralled by this state of perpetually suspended rediscovery. He wants the world to be difficult to see because our understanding leaps too quickly from the *choice* to the *chosen*, from what is *findable* to what is *found*.

Still, the leap is made every second: we act as if we experience the word "because." And if a wide variety of twentieth-century writers stitched their world together with the word "and," interrogating our sense that causality governs the way one thing follows another, we nevertheless tend to make sense of their world by inferring a sense of causality where it has been elided. As a result, a world connected only by "and" may seem simultaneously liberating and disconcerting, the reassertion of a hierarchy of values by apparently neutral means. If Pound's *Cantos* began with the line "Or then went down to the ship" (rather than "And then went down to the ship"), we would be encouraged to imagine a more troubled relationship between the many parts of the poem that follow. If "The Love Song of J. Alfred Prufrock" ended with George Oppen's revision of its final line ("till other voices wake / us or we drown"), we would be encouraged to imagine a future for thought.

Like his modernist forebears, Oppen built his most ambitious poems from an arrangement of fragments whose relationship remains to one degree or another implicit; but by persuading us to think of the parts as connected by "or" rather than "and," Oppen emphasizes the ways in which the parts turn against each other and the whole, interrogating one another. He acknowledges not only the accumulated heap of things but the more threateningly haphazard possibility of their loss. Not coincidentally, Oppen's great subject is the relationship of parts to the whole—the relationship of individuals to the communities that both constitute them and threaten to obliterate them, erasing their strangeness.

In the seventh section of his masterpiece, "Of Being Numerous," Oppen introduces the poem's most important metaphor: the shipwreck, usually associated with Robinson Crusoe, the individual bereft of community.

Obsessed, bewildered

By the shipwreck
Of the singular

We have chosen the meaning
Of being numerous.

Here, Oppen emphasizes the ways in which the community threatens
to neutralize idiosyncratic behavior; it is more difficult to stand alone,
shipwrecked. By saying that Crusoe was "rescued," we eradicate the
productive tension between the part and the whole, having implicitly
chosen to privilege the numerous over "the bright light of shipwreck."
   Jump from the seventh to the thirty-fifth section of the poem,
which begins with the word "or."

   . . . or define
   Man beyond rescue
   of the impoverished, solve
   whole cities

   before we can face
   again
   forests and prairies . . .

Oppen doesn't think that it is possible to live outside of the agreed-
on structures of the community; we must solve the city before we
can think about entering the apparently open spaces of forests and
prairies. But while the poem must be called "Of Being Numerous,"
Oppen insists that the maker of poems "must somehow see the one
thing." We see only by the bright light of shipwreck.
   Or do we? The word "or" does not appear in "Of Being Numerous" with the obsessive frequency with which the word "and"
occurs throughout the *Cantos,* but it is everywhere implicit. Oppen
returns to the shipwreck metaphor in the nineteenth section of the
poem, offering another reading of it.

   Now in the helicopters the casual will
   Is atrocious

Insanity in high places,
If it is true we must do these things
We must cut our throats

The fly in the bottle

Insane, the insane fly

Which, over the city
Is the bright light of shipwreck

Oppen is thinking about Lyndon Johnson's escalation of the Vietnam War, specifically the dropping of napalm from helicopters, whose translucent cockpits he likens to a bottle, the pilot trapped inside to a fly. The trapped fly is in turn associated with the poem's governing metaphor for the individual: the bright light of shipwreck. Here, a metaphor linked to the saving vision of the artist is now associated with the dropping of liquid fire on children.

Or is it? Oppen borrowed the metaphor of the trapped fly from the *Philosophical Investigations:* "What is your aim in philosophy," Wittgenstein asks himself, and the answer is, "To shew the fly the way out of the fly-bottle." Oppen wants similarly to release the part from the whole, but like Wittgenstein he recognizes that we may do so only by erecting more elaborate poems, more elaborate communities— more bottles from which we might release more flies. As a result, the whole of "Of Being Numerous" turns on Oppen's willingness not only to interrogate his own convictions but to suffer their collapse as well. "The isolated man is dead," says Oppen, turning against his vision of the artist who must see only one thing. "The isolated man is dead, his world around him exhausted // And he fails! He fails, that meditative man! And indeed they cannot 'bear' it." Oppen wants to bear failure, bear it willingly, openly. The poet who lives by the light of shipwreck may also find himself trapped in the fly bottle.

The relationship between these two metaphors is everything: how exactly should they be linked? To say that one were a peacock *and* a peony would, in Proust's world, distract our attention from the temporal process of transformation, the visceral process of thought. To say that one were a visionary poet *and* an insane pilot would recuse us from the obligation of asking more questions. For as much as the poet's vision and the pilot's vision might resemble each other, they are not exactly the same thing. We know how to move forward depending on the syntax we employ, and if the word "because" puts one foot purposefully in front of the other, if the word "and" permits us to wander, the word "or" forces us to stagger, doubling backward, falling down. "Or" is our means of defending ourselves against our own strength.

VIII. *Leaving Things Out*

ERNEST HEMINGWAY JUSTIFIED the cryptic flatness of stories like "Big Two-Hearted River" by proposing that "you could omit anything if you knew that you omitted." This remark makes us self-conscious about something that all texts do, no matter how lucid their designs. Recall the work of the Shakespeare scholar A. C. Bradley, who asked the maligned but unforgettable question, "How many children had Lady Macbeth?" If Bradley seems to be spinning his wheels, it is only because the answer to his question doesn't carry a great deal of weight. Consider another question: why is Antonio sad at the beginning of *The Merchant of Venice?*

> In sooth I know not why I am so sad,
> It wearies me, you say it wearies you;
> But how I caught it, found it, or came by it,
> What stuff 'tis made of, whereof it is born,
> I am to learn.

These are the opening lines of the play, and just as Antonio is to learn, so are the other characters in the play—and so is the play's audience. Solerio and Solanio propose (and by doing so raise the play's two important categories) first that Antonio is sad about money and second that he is sad about love. Antonio denies both reasons, suggesting, somewhat predictably, that the world is "a stage, where every man must play a part, / And mine a sad one."

Solerio and Solanio accept this explanation, but readers of *The Merchant of Venice* cannot; Shakespeare's use of the world-as-stage cliché almost seems meant to direct us from the action of the play to the action of our experience of the play. Antonio starts out sad, gets sadder, has reason to be cheered up, but nevertheless ends the play alone, surrounded by couples, as sad as he was in act 1. In pursuit of an explanation for Antonio's sadness, readers have gone to lengths that make Bradley's seem modest, and my purpose is not to lengthen the debate. When Freud admits provocatively in *The Interpretation of Dreams* that "the essence of the dream-thoughts need not be represented in the dream at all," he is not describing a special case but emphasizing the interpreter's responsibility for constructing that essence from cryptic and overdetermined evidence. The job of interpretation—what in fact we're doing when we interpret—is to supply what the poem has appeared to omit, and our continuing interest in a poem turns on its resistance to our efforts.

Some poems do make us pointedly aware of our job: these lines from Jorie Graham's "Untitled Two" read like a dream in which the essence of the dream is not represented.

> And then one girl, like a stairway appearing in the exhausted light,
> remembers the *reason* with a fast sharp gasp,
> and laughter rises, bending, from the chalice of five memories,
> as they move past us towards the railing of the lot,
> one stepping over, quick, one leaping high, giggling—red hair above
> her
>   as she
> drops—two whispering, one hands in pockets looking down
> as she, most carefully, leans into the quick step
> over the silver rail—oh bright forgetting place—then
> skips to catch up with the rest,
> and the rail gleams, and the rail overflows with corrugated light.

Graham describes the movement of several teen-aged girls through a congested parking lot. The cars "gather round, gloat, tangle, clot," and their drivers are a "gigantic sum of zeros that won't add." In contrast to this unassimilated hoard of nameless people, the girls seem liberated: they move freely, speaking to one another. But if "Untitled Two" dramatizes the idea of a shared inner life, that idea remains elusive. We see the girls laughing and whispering; we feel the metaphysical weight of Graham's metaphors for these actions ("like a stairway appearing in the exhausted light"), and we experience the rush of movement embodied in her effortlessly convoluted syntax. But we never know what the "reason" motivating these clearly rendered actions might be: we feel the powerful presence of an inner logic but the poem does not name it.

At the center of *The Errancy*, the book that contains "Untitled Two," lies "Le Manteau de Pascal," a meditation on the coat in which Pascal was buried—the coat in which Pascal's sister sewed the philosopher's never-revealed proof of the existence of God. At the center of the poem is a line that will be repeated four times: "You do understand, don't you, by looking?" With each repetition the question seems less rhetorical, more urgent. It registers not only an awareness of how little we have understood but also the conviction that all we can do is look again: whatever we know about the spirit within the body, the meaning within the poem, we know as surface, an exterior. "Dreams are nothing other than a particular *form* of thinking," said Freud, emphasizing that the surface is all an interpreter knows: "It is the *dream-work* which creates that form, and it alone is the essence of dreaming." Throughout *The Errancy* Graham weaves a vividly sensuous surface—a coat—enticing us with the possibility of a reason without necessarily positing it. "It has a fine inner lining," says Graham, "but it is / as an exterior that you see it."

To say that a poem wears its essence like a coat might seem like a justification of a concertedly abstruse manner of writing, but in fact the same thing may be said of the pointedly lucid poems of Elizabeth Bishop.

> A small bus comes along, in up-and-down rushes,
> packed with people, even to its step.
> (On weekdays with groceries, spare automobile parts, and pump parts,
> but today only two preachers extra, one carrying his frock coat on a hanger.)
> It passes the closed roadside stand, the closed schoolhouse,
> where today no flag is flying
> from the rough-adzed pole topped with a white china doorknob.
> It stops, and a man carrying a baby gets off,

climbs over a stile, and goes down through a small steep meadow,
which establishes its poverty in a snowfall of daisies,
to his invisible house beside the water.

The birds keep on singing, a calf bawls, the bus starts.
The thin mist follows
the white mutations of its dream;
an ancient chill is rippling the dark brooks.

In the thirty-nine lines that precede these final stanzas of "Cape Breton," no human presence enters the landscape. Although it is Sunday, the churches are empty; bulldozers stand idle. But rather than offering a respite from this quizzical sense of emptiness, the emergence of people in the landscape exacerbates it. The priest isn't wearing his vestments—why? The glimpse of a man carrying a baby seems to promise a depth of human feeling, yet he disappears to an "invisible house"—a house that the lay of the land won't allow us to see but that feels literally invisible. Singing birds and bawling calves seem only more or less as animated as the moving bus: everything in the landscape is shrouded equally in a mist that seems to be the most motivated presence in the landscape even as it empties the landscape of interiority.

Despite its clarity, "Cape Breton" is a poem of terrified desperation: it records a sequence of failed attempts to locate human meaning in a landscape that sloughs us off. Like "Le Manteau de Pascal," it acknowledges that we know only the surface of things, but at the same time it admits that we crave depth. "Whatever the landscape had of meaning appears to have been abandoned," says Bishop, who immediately posits an "interior" she cannot see: an interior

where deep lakes are reputed to be,
and disused trails and mountains of rock
and miles of burnt forests standing in gray scratches
like the admirable scriptures made on stones by stones—
and these regions now have little to say for themselves
except in thousands of light song-sparrow songs floating upward
freely, dispassionately, through the mist, and meshing
in brown-wet, fine, torn fish-nets.

Nothing Bishop describes here (lakes, trails, mountains, burnt forests, sparrows, fishnets) exists. This passage is a catalog of what she presumes the surface of the landscape is holding back in its "interior," the figment of an imagination that needs desperately to affirm its own interiority by positing an essence in the world outside. If Bishop seems initially like a poet who feels certain that we understand simply by looking, the ultimate effect of her poem depends on the absence of what we crave.

What is left out of this landscape?

> The day is come when I again repose
> Here, under this dark sycamore, and view
> These plots of cottage-ground, these orchard-tufts,
> Which, at this season, with their unripe fruits,
> Among the woods and copses lose themselves,
> Nor, with their green and simple hue, disturb
> The wild green landscape. Once again I see
> These hedge-rows, hardly hedge-rows, little lines
> Of sportive wood run wild, these pastoral farms,
> Green to the very door; and wreaths of smoke
> Sent up, in silence, from among the trees,
> With some uncertain notice, as might seem,
> Of vagrant dwellers in the houseless woods,
> Or of some hermit's cave, where by his fire
> The hermit sits alone.

These lines are located, as they themselves insist, *here:* under a dark sycamore. Nothing "disturbs" the "wild green landscape." But when Wordsworth revisited it in 1798, Tintern Abbey was a refuge for homeless beggars and the wretchedly poor; the landscape around it was scarred by the early excesses of the industrial revolution. Only a little of that historical evidence appears in Wordsworth's poem ("wreaths of smoke" sent up "as might seem / Of vagrant dwellers in the houseless woods, / Or of some hermit's cave"), but that evidence, combined with the fact that the poem's title skirts the anniversary of Bastille Day ("Lines written a few miles above Tintern Abbey, on revisiting the Banks of the Wye during a Tour, July 13, 1798"), persuades the literary critic Marjorie Levinson to conclude that "what we witness in this poem is a conversion of public to private property, history to poetry." Jerome McGann speaks similarly of the poem's "displacement" of social conditions, then of "erasures and displacements," and finally of "annihilation": "the poem annihilates its history."

This argument equates displacement with omission; however, Freud is adamant in *The Interpretation of Dreams* that displacement is the opposite of omission: it is the means by which repression is subverted, allowing forbidden thoughts to be admitted into a dream. We approach *The Merchant of Venice* with a question (Why is Antonio sad?) and with the help of what evidence is available, we postulate an answer. We approach "Tintern Abbey" with a question (Why is Wordsworth sad?) and postulate a similar kind of answer. The first answer depends on our using evidence to fabricate a missing world of plot and character motivation; the second depends on our using evidence to fabricate a missing world of historical context and authorial motivation. To suggest that by omitting a clear delineation of place the poem converts history to poetry is to presume omission to be repression—a problematic rather than an inevitable aspect of a text. It is to suggest that because language has a complex relationship to what it represents, there must be something better than the language of poetry—a more reliable way to insure that the location of a poem is contained in the poem. It is to ask the poem to be useful so that it might never be useful enough.

Poems often take place in identifiable locations, many of them literal, some of them historically verifiable. "Cape Breton" takes place at Cape Breton, "Untitled Two" in a parking lot. But if the named location of "Tintern Abbey" seems in danger of disappearing, the locations of Bishop's and Graham's poems feel increasingly less present. Does this trajectory represent the attenuation of a remediable problem or the recognition of the problem's complexity—a complexity inherent in the language of Wordsworth's poem?

In *Swarm,* the book that followed *The Errancy,* Jorie Graham pushes the problem further. "Locations are omitted," she pronounces on the book's first page, and the poems that follow don't seem to be happening anywhere, not even in a parking lot.

> What are you thinking?
> Here on the bottom?

What do you squint clear for yourself
up there through the surface?

Explain   door ajar.
Explain   hopeth all.
Explain   surface   future   subject-of.

Pierce.

Be swift.

(Let's wade again.)

(Offstage: pointing-at)
(Offstage: stones placing themselves on eyes)

Here: tangle and seaweed

current   diagram   how deep?   I have

forgotten.

Don't leave me. I won't.

These lines from "For One Must Want / To Shut the Other's Gaze"
are located, as they themselves insist, *here:* on the bottom of the ocean,
beneath the surface, among tangle and seaweed. But imagining that
location doesn't help us to read the poem; like most of the poems of
Swarm, it feels challengingly disembodied, all cry and no occasion—
as if we were asked to imagine the interior space below the surface
without any knowledge of the surface. More helpful is the fact that
the poem's title is a misquotation from Emily Dickinson's "I cannot
live with You," a poem about the intensity of being merged with
the beloved. "Explain door ajar," says Graham. "So we must meet
apart—/ You there—I—here—/ With just the Door ajar / That Oceans
are," says Dickinson, emphasizing that a perfect unity of lover and
beloved destroys the distance on which the passion of love depends.
The "here" of Graham's poem is more richly understood as this
metaphorical ocean rather than a literal one; it is a place of almost
unbearable union that paradoxically preserves distinctions, a place
where the merging of selves creates not understanding but a craving
for explanation. And in its final lines, the poem honors that craving

even as it refuses to satisfy it: while insisting that "the real plot was invisible" it also asks us to "name the place." As if to stress that we've come to this poem not for knowledge but for the experience of what it feels like to know something, "For One Must Want / To Shut the Other's Gaze" concludes with the question with which it began: "What are you thinking?"

If it seems fair to say that "For One Must Want / To Shut the Other's Gaze" has all but omitted a location, how is it different from any poem that might be said to convert "history to poetry" by giving insufficient attention to the particular details of its place? As if to raise this question, Graham followed *Swarm* with *Never,* a book in which she returns relentlessly to identifiable locations. "How can I believe in that?" asked Keats when he first saw the Lake District he had come to know from Wordsworth's poems. This question is the epigraph to *Never,* and the poems represent a massively patient attempt simply to record the tone of things as they appear in particular locations at particular times. "Over a dock railing, I watch the minnows," begins the first poem in the book.

But this resolve breeds new questions: having made the decision to record the object world as faithfully as possible, locating the object in space and time, how does one evade the temporality of the act of recording? In "Gulls" Graham stares at ocean water on a sandy beach; to call it a "wave" is to foreclose questions the poem needs to entertain.

> So then it's sun in surf-breaking water: incircling, smearing: mind
> not
> knowing if it's still "wave," breaking on
> itself, small glider, or if it's "amidst" (red turning feathery)
> or rather "over" (the laciness of foambreak) or just *what*—(among
> the line of also smearingly reddening terns floating out now
> on the feathery backedge of foambroken
> looking)—*it is.*

What it is: Graham is focused "head-down and over some one / thing" throughout these lines as throughout the whole of *Never,* but her devotion does not guarantee a confidant rendition of the object world. She craves the certainty of location, but each wave passes, becomes some other thing, no sooner glimpsed than gone.

What's more, the rendered wave becomes a figure for the poet's language, which also exists in a constant state of flux, its drive to predication constantly diverted. If locations were omitted from the poems of *Swarm,* how should they be said to have been included in *Never?*

In "For One Must Want / To Shut the Other's Gaze" language feels less determinedly referential than in "Tintern Abbey," but the poem is not written in a different language. A poem may make us more or less aware of the intricate relationship of words to things, however, and in this sense "For One Must Want / To Shut the Other's Gaze" foregrounds the complexity of any poem's relationship to its place. All poems are troubled about their own locations because their language is troubled by its referentiality; they recognize that the effort to include a clear sense of a location in the poem may become indistinguishable from the effort to omit it.

To wonder about a poem's conversion of history to poetry is consequently to reiterate poetry's long-standing resistance to itself. "What can music do / Against the weapons of soldiers," asks a shepherd in Virgil's ninth eclogue, disrupting our appreciation of what Wordsworth called the wild green landscape. "Soldier, there is a war," says Wallace Stevens in the coda to "Notes toward a Supreme Fiction," turning against his vision of a perfectly turned world—"my green, my fluent mundo." The poem confronts itself with what it has so far appeared to omit.

> Soldier, there is a war between the mind
> And sky, between thought and day and night. It is
> For that the poet is always in the sun,
>
> Patches the moon together in his room
> To his Virgilian cadences, up down,
> Up down. It is a war that never ends.
>
> Yet it depends on yours. The two are one.
> They are a plural, a right and left, a pair,
> Two parallels that meet if only in
>
> The meeting of their shadows or that meet
> In a book in a barrack, a letter from Malay.

For the poet, the war is a metaphor; for the soldier it is not. The poet's war "between the mind / And sky" takes place "in his room," and if this war meets the soldier's war it is only in "a book in a barrack, a letter from Malay"—only, that is, in the brief moments when the intimacy afforded by language intersects with a war that is, as Stevens said elsewhere, emphasizing the limitations of poetry in a time of social crisis, "a military state of affairs, not a literary one."

Many readers have found the coda to "Notes" jarring or dissatisfying—as if Wordsworth had appended lines to "Tintern Abbey" in which he admitted that he felt miserably unsure of what shape social responsibility should take in the aftermath of the French Revolution. Some readers ignore the coda because they want to question the poem's apparent suppression of its location; others ignore the coda because they want to celebrate the poem's apparent transcendence of its location. But a reading of "Notes toward a Supreme Fiction" that capitalizes on the poem's metaphors of harmony, ignoring the intrusion of its wartime coda, would make as little sense as a reading of *The Merchant of Venice* that ignores the Shylock plot, accepting gratefully the play's invocation of social harmony. For if the bulk of "Notes toward a Supreme Fiction" implicitly justifies an evasive poetry in the face of an endlessly evasive world, the poem's coda insists that this justification of endless resistance must itself be resisted. Or, to put it another way, if the poem implicitly suggests that no one really wants to face a world at war, the epilogue suddenly reminds us that we must face it, just as the poem must end. Rather than evading the epilogue, we need to feel its challenge—its recognition of the intricate ways in which evasion is complicit with confrontation, omission with inclusion.

Anxiety about what a text omits is finally an anxiety about figurative language: does a metaphor repress the thing to which it refers or is it the means by which repression is subverted? "Notes toward a Supreme Fiction" is troubled by this question, but it doesn't entertain the notion that a poem could make the question go away by ceasing to employ figurative language; the poem lives in the question. Nor does the poem congratulate itself for employing figurative language subversively, smuggling the repressed into poetry. Poems may sometimes encourage us to think this way, but poems also make us question this way of thinking: to rest comfortably on a poem's discomfort with itself is to evade an anxiety that poems by Wordsworth,

Stevens, Bishop, and Graham cannot help but amplify because the language of poetry amplifies it. So while poems cannot help but leave things out, and while the job of interpretation is in some sense to supply what the poem has appeared to omit, we return to poems when they make our job difficult. Poems show us how it feels to like trouble.

IX. *Composed Wonder*

"IT IS OWING TO THEIR WONDER, " said Aristotle in the *Meta-physics,* "that people both now begin and at first began to philoso-phize." Wonder is the reinvention of humility, the means by which we fall in love with the world. We gaze at the moon. We read a poem we've read a hundred times before. "People do not feel towards strangers as they do towards their own countrymen, and the same thing is true of their feeling for language. It is therefore well to give everyday speech an unfamiliar air: people like what strikes them, and are struck by what is out of the way." Aristotle makes this remark in the *Rhetoric* by way of justifying the traditional hierarchy of styles, particularly the use of highly figurative language in poetic drama. But the remark also suggests that to enter the space of language is in any case to have made the event strange, to have alienated us from the event so that we might be liberated to discover its wonder. We are no longer free to be bored because we can no longer be knowing; we are humbled.

Wonder is most commonly associated with youth. It thrives on ignorance, inexperience, and firstness; its enemies are knowledge, memory, and repetition. Think of *The Tempest,* when Miranda (whose name means wonder) gazes on human beings other than her father: "O brave new world," she exclaims; " 'tis new to thee," her father adds. Is his knowingness jaded or wise? Is her wonder naive or wounding? What if there can be nothing new, asks Shakespeare in the fifty-ninth sonnet, aware that the question itself is not new.

> If there be nothing new, but that which is
> Hath been before, how are our brains beguiled,
> Which, lab'ring for invention, bear amiss

The second burden of a former child?
O that record could with a backward look
Ev'n of five hundred courses of the sun,
Show me your image in some antique book,
Since mind at first in character was done,
That I might see what the old world could say
To this composed wonder of your frame;
Whether we are mended, or where better they,
Or whether revolution be the same.
    O sure I am the wits of former days
    To subjects worse have giv'n admiring praise.

If there is, as Ecclesiastes maintains, no new thing under the sun, then why does the poet labor to find new ways to describe the beauty of the beloved? How is the brain beguiled into thinking that old, familiar words are born again? Shakespeare begins this sonnet by seeming to want to answer this question, but the sonnet does not really provide an answer: it is all for beguilement—for the poetic means by which something repeated thousands of times may nonetheless enthrall us.

If, the sonnet continues, there is indeed nothing new, then the beauty of the beloved has existed forever. We might see his beauty in a book written at the very moment when writing itself was first invented, when the mind was first done "in character." We might discover what this "old world" said in response to the "composed wonder" of the beloved's "frame," a word that cuts two ways. Most plainly, the frame is the beloved's body, and the poet wonders how the very first writers of poems might have responded to its composed wonder. More important, the frame is the sonnet itself, and the poet wonders how the very first writers might now respond to its composed wonder. The sonnet's final lines return to the opening question, providing a sequence of choices linked with "or" (if we knew the past we could know if we are better writers, worse, or the same) and then following the choices with an assertion that overrides them. But the sonnet turns on the force of the phrase "composed wonder," asserting that we are rightly beguiled out of our knowingness by the power of language.

This wonder is contingent not on a recovery of ignorance, as if such a thing were possible, but on the recognition that knowledge is beside the point. Reading this sonnet, we feel its wonder not simply because we are struck by its argument, never to be so struck again, but because the shape of the argument, how it is composed, gives us pleasure. "Syntax and grammar are the enemies of wonder," ventures Phillip Fisher, and we live nowhere but in time, in repetition, in syntax—in the temporal structures that guarantee our mortality. The very things that resist wonder must also be the things on which wonder depends, or else we could never feel it. Wonder contingent on inexperience and firstness can be easy to feel, and the challenge is to be wounded by "composed wonder"—wonder produced by poetry's mechanisms of self-resistance: syntax, line, figurative language, disjunction, spokenness. Without these mechanisms, poems would be vehicles for knowledge, explanations of experience that would threaten to dispel its wonder. They would be useful, then disposable.

Sometimes, of course, they are. Sometimes we feel like the Baudelaire driven by boredom and spleen, for whom everything leads to nothing; at other times we feel like the Baudelaire for whom everything is a metaphor, every sensation leading through other words to other worlds. Sometimes the final scene of *The Tempest* will leave us cold, and we will point to reasons why we might feel that way, from the actor playing Prospero to the wine we drank with lunch. Another time, the final scene might move us as never before. Even more hair-raising, because we have nowhere else to turn, is our private encounter with the language on the page. If we are bored, is our knowingness jaded or wise? If we are enthralled, is our wonder wounding or naive? We may not know for sure, but the only way to approach these questions is to read the poem again, not ever for the first time. If the poem is resisting itself strenuously enough, then chances are that our own resistance to the poem will be overwhelmed. The language will give us pleasure because it gives us work to do, work that can never be completed no matter how fully explained the poem might be.

Louise Glück's poem "Nostos" (the Greek word for homecoming) is about this kind of infinitely repeatable work. And inasmuch as it doesn't pretend to teach us anything new about the fact that we grow old, the poem resists a feeling of wonder. But "Nostos" also enacts this process in a drama of syntax. "There was an apple tree in the yard," it begins flatly, adding a smattering of details whose relevance it is difficult to judge: crocuses, damp grass, flowers in the neighbors' yard. In retrospect, the poem continues, the apple tree seemed to flower magically on the poet's birthday, year after year, but the poem also acknowledges that such an apparently magical event could only have happened once.

> How many times, really, did the tree
> flower on my birthday,
> the exact day, not
> before, not after? Substitution
> of the immutable
> for the shifting, the evolving.
> Substitution of the image
> for relentless earth. What
> do I know of this place,
> the role of the tree for decades
> taken by a bonsai, voices
> rising from the tennis courts—
> Fields. Smell of the tall grass, new cut.
> As one expects of a lyric poet.
> We look at the world once, in childhood.
> The rest is memory.

This poem acknowledges the fact that memory is the enemy of wonder, but the temporal unfolding of the poem's syntax makes this act of acknowledgment feel wonderful: we are led through a tranquil assortment of recollections until the unexpectedly adamant conclusion of the poem suddenly transforms the assortment into a straight line. On the one hand, the poem describes the inexorable way in which our desires ride on rails that were laid down years ago: this is the potentially disheartening sense of the line "as one expects of a lyric poet." On the other hand, the poem makes the act of discovering this line feel immensely uplifting: the movement of the poem, hesitant enjambments finally giving way to three lines in which syntax and line coincide, makes the mind's work feel dynamic, full of possibility. To say that "the rest is memory" might mean that we are doomed merely to repeat the past, or it might mean that we are liberated from the past—free to forget the facts in order to remake ourselves in the future. In either case, our experience of the poem's movement is always an act of discovery, no matter if the poem is as familiar to us as leaves on a tree. The homecoming of "Nostos" is not a return to a place we've always known but the discovery of a place we've always known but never truly seen.

One has only to imagine a poem beginning with the line "We look at the world once, in childhood" to realize how the effect of "Nostos" is produced by its composition rather than its event. The poem lives not by its wisdom, which we already know anyway, but by enacting the discovery of its wisdom, which is infinitely repeatable as a pattern of intonation and stress. Neither is its wonder dispelled by explanation, since the final three lines are somewhat explanatory in relationship to the lines preceding them. But the explanation is arranged so that our discovery of it is itself beguiling. We feel the movement from heavily enjambed lines to syntactically closed lines, from image-freighted lines ("voices / rising from the tennis courts— / Fields") to lines of abstract statement ("The rest is memory"). In this poem, syntax and memory are wonder's best enemies.

In the final lines of Anthony Hecht's " 'It Out-Herods Herod. Pray You, Avoid It,' " the enemies are meter and rhyme.

> Yet by quite other laws
> My children make their case;
> Half God, half Santa Claus,
> But with my voice and face,
>
> A hero comes to save
> The poorman, beggarman, thief,
> And make the world behave
> And put an end to grief.
>
> And that their sleep be sound
> I say this childermas
> Who could not, at one time,
> Have saved them from the gas.

Throughout this poem's nine trimeter quatrains, Hecht watches his children watching a TV Western. If the children believe that good will triumph over evil in their lives as on the screen, Hecht sees himself not as the benevolent hero but as the "giant" set to "bust out of the clink" when the children have gone to bed. And though by the end of the poem we have become quite used to the aural pleasure of these rhymes, something astonishing happens in the final quatrain: the content of its last line ("Have saved them from the gas") is potentially overpowering. Nothing in the preceding eight stanzas prepares us for it, and even if the Holocaust seems in retrospect to be everywhere in " 'It Out-Herods Herod. Pray You, Avoid It,' " the poem's final lines continue to surprise. When we hear the first half of the final stanza ("And that their sleep be sound / I say this childermas") we are fully prepared for the aural experience of the stanza clicking into place with a rhyme on "childermas." We don't necessarily expect the poem to jump to a new register ("Who could not, at one time, / Have saved them from the gas"), but the expected rhyme makes the leap seem horribly inevitable. Because of the final line's rhyme, we feel the sudden weight of historical aftermath. The effect is both delicate and momentous, for if the power of the poem were staked on its content alone, the Holocaust would seem dangerously like a prize, the poet's attempt to purchase our attention for his poem. It would "out-Herod" Herod, as Hamlet cautions the players not to do in their performance of the play within *Hamlet*.

"First wonder," says the poet J. V. Cunningham in his study of Shakespearean tragedy, "then explanation." That is a succinct account of the way many of the tragedies end. In their final lines, someone steps out to explain what has transpired, picking up the pieces. But inasmuch as these passages convert wonder into knowledge, they have only to do with the wonder of events, not the wonder of language, which cannot be dispelled by explanation. "In an *explained* universe," says the philosopher E. M. Cioran, "nothing would still have a meaning, except madness itself. A thing we have encompassed no longer counts." Even this remark, more hostile to explanation, is not fully relevant to what Shakespeare calls "composed" wonder. For the wonder of language depends less on meaning than on the ways in which it means, the shape of the temporal process we negotiate in the act of reading or writing a poem.

The event invoked in the final line of " 'It Out-Herods Herod' " is more threatening than Glück's vision of a blossoming apple tree, but to have said so is to have said nothing about either poem's claim on our attention over time. Wonder is to be distinguished from the sublime, suggests Fisher, because the sublime is the aestheticization of fear while wonder is the aestheticization of delight. Sometimes the two are difficult to disentangle; Horatio is harrowed by both "fear and wonder" when he sees the ghost of Hamlet's father in the opening scene of the play. But fear is more readily dissipated by explanation: once we understand what we fear, we have mastered it and are no longer quite so susceptible to its mystery. Objects of wonder must remain perpetually unnamable if their power is to be relished repeatedly, and the language of great poems will resist our mastery long after we have explained the events they happen to be about. Even to translate the event into language is to create, as Aristotle suggests, a space amenable to wonder; it is the space created by the work of figurative language, the work of seeing one thing in terms of another. Poems reawaken us to the pleasure of the unintelligibility of the world.

Of course any piece of writing has the potential to do that.

> An immense tea-tray, august, its voice filling the black circle of the horizon, thundered to the ground. Numerous pieces of sheet-iron said, "Pack. Pack. Pack." In minutes the clay floor of the hut shook, the drums of ears were pressed inward, solid noise showered about the universe, enormous echoes pushed these men—to the right, to the left, or down toward the tables, and crackling like that of flames among vast underwood became the settled condition of the night. Catching the light from the brazier as the head leaned over, the lips of one of the two men on the floor were incredibly red and full and went on talking and talking.

This is the second paragraph of *No More Parades,* the second novel in *Parade's End,* Ford Madox Ford's tetralogy of novels about the First World War. As we read further, we deduce what has happened here: a hut containing Welsh, English, and Canadian soldiers has been shelled. But Ford's narration creates a dynamic impression of the event as it happens rather than a retrospective account; the paragraph's metaphors simultaneously disguise the actual event and convey more vividly the experience of its horror. Reading the paragraph, we participate in the confusion of the human consciousness that the language renders implicitly. And we register something about an Edwardian mind that, in its confusion, would fall back on *Alice in Wonderland,* apprehending exploding shells as a giant, clattering tea tray.

Ford's prose edges toward the kind of writing we call "poetic" because far from taking the power of figurative language for granted, Ford highlights it, asking us to linger in the space between the actual event (the exploding shells) and the composition of the event in language (the falling tea tray). Poems tend to capitalize on this space in a variety of ways. Most obviously, poems that eschew an orderly narrative in favor of a disjunctive array of images tend to traffic most plainly in wonder; in their strength, such poems feel enticing, no matter how opaque their surfaces. But as the work of Glück and Hecht suggests in different ways, poems also capitalize on this space by dramatizing our discovery of it within the temporal unfolding of the poem. To feel the eruption of wonder convincingly, we need to feel an equally convincing lack of wonder; the effect depends on a movement from one psychic state to another. We wouldn't want to live in a continuous state of wonder even if we could, since what we relish is not necessarily wonder as such but the unpredictable wave of wonder rising from the texture of ordinary experience, making it strange. So if we need to cultivate a sense of wonder in order to reinvigorate our relationship with the world, we also need to lose a sense of wonder in order to fall in love with the world again.

To dread the absence of wonder is to live constantly in need of fresh stimulation. It is to remain forever a child, to refuse mortality. Wonder may become "the exhilaration of a mourning that never gives up hope," says Adam Phillips, the refusal "to take contingency seriously," and the same charge could be brought against poems that promise to be wonderful forever. For if one danger is the poem whose language does not return us to the world's unintelligibility, another is the poem that embraces the unintelligible so single-mindedly that there is nothing to be lost. If the resistance to poetry is the wonder of poetry, how do we prevent resistance from becoming a fetish, something with which we are merely fascinated?

Recall the final scenes of *The Winter's Tale*. Hermione and her daughter Perdita have been presumed dead for sixteen years, condemned by the jealous Leontes. Paulina has kept Hermione in hiding, however, and once Perdita is found, Paulina dramatizes her mistress's rebirth through the power of art. "I like your silence," she says to the dumbstruck Leontes while unveiling an astonishingly lifelike statue of Hermione: "it the more shows off / Your wonder." So filled with wonder is Perdita that she stands "like stone" before the statue, which is itself merely "like stone"; the statue is in fact Hermione posing as a work of art.

Like *The Tempest*, *The Winter's Tale* is as much about the dissipation of wonder as about its delight. For when Paulina commands the statue of Hermione to move, bringing the work of art to life, she dispels wonder with "more amazement." The spell is broken by the recognition that there is no spell; fascination gives way to warm embrace. And in its final moments, this play we've come to call a romance ends with unanswered questions rather than the explanations more common to the tragedies: "Where has thou been preserv'd? where lived? how found / Thy father's court," Hermione asks her long-lost daughter Perdita, herself an object of wonder. "There's time enough for that," answers Paulina, and while the line suggests that explanations will eventually be provided, it also reminds us that we live in time: whatever is found will be lost again. *The Winter's Tale* is a parable about art's great power to compose wonder, but the parable also suggests that our greatest loss is to be forever dazzled by the parable itself.

Wonder matters because we must ultimately become unable to bear it. We leave the theater, we return to the ordinary world, so that we might again feel bored with ourselves. If we are Baudelaire, we find it as necessary to dramatize our blankness as to dramatize our fascination with a glistening strand of hair. If we are Wallace Stevens, we become connoisseurs of the dissipation of wonder, intent on rediscovering the poverty of the soul and the inability of language to transport us beyond a life of dull routine. If we are Louise Glück, we come to accept these routines with an almost inhuman stoicism. "There is in these rituals something apart from wonder," she says in "Solstice," before taking the next step, scrutinizing our stake in the loss of wonder as stringently as she has interrogated our craving for it: "there is also a kind of preening, / as though human genius had participated in these arrangements / and we found the results satisfying." A stoic acceptance of the loss of wonder is as limiting as the inability to bear the loss, and the point is that we may rest nowhere.

In the middle of her long poem "October," Glück tells the story of a child's first entrancement with the otherness of the natural world. Nothing is learned here; the child is awakened to the mystery of what she is not.

Come to me, said the world.
This is not to say
it spoke in exact sentences
but that I perceived beauty in this manner.

Sunrise. A film of moisture
on each living thing. Pools of cold light
formed in the gutters.

I stood
at the doorway,
ridiculous as it now seems.

What others found in art,
I found in nature. What others found
in human love, I found in nature.
Very simple. But there was no voice there.

Winter was over. In the thawed dirt,
bits of green were showing.

Come to me, said the world. I was standing
in my wool coat at a kind of bright portal—
I can finally say
long ago; it gives me considerable pleasure.

While these lines present a paradigmatic discovery of wonder (de-
pendant on youth, ignorance, inexperience, firstness), the lines themselves seem unimpressed with that discovery. If the world once
seemed to speak, Glück is stern in her rejection of the metaphor
of inhuman speech. If she felt that the world beyond the threshold
was new, the idea now seems ridiculous. If that feeling, however
ridiculous, was contingent on her youth, she is no longer young: this
happened long ago.

What's more, inasmuch as this singular event is composed within
the language of the poem, it happens more than once. Not once but
twice the world says "*Come to me*" for the first time. Twice does the
poem insist that the world did not really speak. Twice does it say
that the illusion of an answering voice was found in nature rather

than in art or love. Twice does the child stand in a doorway or bright portal. By its very composition, this poem insists that this feeling of wonder is not to be reclaimed, and yet, despite its scrupulousness, the poem feels hungry for the feeling. Glück's repetitions distance us from the child's astonishment but also serve to make that astonishment available, as if the drama of the poem were to try, having failed once, to compose the feeling in language again. To describe the child's threshold experience as taking place first "at the doorway" and then "at a kind of bright portal" is to open the space of wonder in language even as the repetition forecloses the wonder of the event, undermining its singularity. To insist again that "there was no voice there" is to make us wonder more deeply about the source of the invocation. To dwell on the "film of moisture" on each living thing is to emphasize the allure of ordinary things that seem different from themselves, just as the phrase "bright portal" makes the doorway feel provocative again.

Everything happens after something else in "October": the poem's title invokes the world after the terrorist attacks of September 11, 2001. After such violence, Glück asks, how can we entertain the possibility of wonder again? That we will entertain it seems to her certain; in our weakness or our strength, we will crave the feeling. But if it seems ridiculous to remember how earnestly we once stood on the threshold of experience, how will we reinvigorate our sense of wonder without seeming not only ridiculous but irresponsible? How do we prevent our desire to fall in love with the world from disguising a need to be protected from its ugliness? How do we prevent wonder from becoming a bereaved fascination with a world to which we no longer have access?

The questions themselves are not new. "The war, people said, had revived their interest in poetry," remarked Virginia Woolf after the First World War, and "October" is written in the wake of a similar revival. "The songs of morning sound over-rehearsed," says Glück, aware that her own poem is made of a tissue of repetitions, aware that we will want to hear the word "mourning" where she offers a more troublingly neutral word. The songs are "still quite beautiful," but so are the "long shadows of the maples / nearly mauve on the gravel paths." Summer warmth repeats itself in "October," returning as if nothing had happened in September. "It does me no good," says

Glück more than once, and poems feel similarly beside the point, no matter how beautiful or timely their consolation. Why do some people keep reading and writing them?

"It is true there is not enough beauty in the world," Glück admits in prosaic, end-stopped lines. "It is also true that I am not competent to restore it." In the heavily enjambed lines that follow, she nonetheless continues to work.

> I am
> at work, though I am silent.
>
> The bland
>
> misery of the world
> bounds us on either side, an alley
>
> lined with trees; we are
>
> companions here, not speaking,
> each with his own thoughts;
>
> behind the trees, iron
> gates of the private houses,
> the shuttered rooms
>
> somehow deserted, abandoned,
>
> as though it were the artist's
> duty to create
> hope, but out of what? what?
>
> the word itself
> false, a device to refute
> perception— At the intersection,
>
> ornamental lights of the season.
>
> I was young here. Riding
> the subway with my small book
> as though to defend myself against
>
> this same world:

> *you are not alone,*
> the poem said,
> in the dark tunnel.

Glück's sense of her powerlessness is acute here. The poet is as isolated as any human being, trapped by circumstance, bounded by misery. What's worse, the misery is experienced as duty. And the obligation to create something new feels not only irrelevant but also presumptuous: how can hope be entertained when the word itself feels like a temptation to divert our eyes from suffering, a device to refute perception?

Glück needs to transform this dead end into an intersection, and she does so literally, shifting the poem abruptly from a discursive account of the poet's dilemma to another remembered experience of youth: "At the intersection, // ornamental lights of the season." The lights immediately suggest promise, but they are (like everything in "October") seasonal, a repeated gesture rather than a uniquely wonderful experience. Neither is the act of reading a book on a subway train unique; it has happened before and will happen again. Surrounded by people, the reader feels alone. The book is small, and the act of reading is private, unshared. The poems have no power to heal other people's misery, but in contrast to the overwhelmingly massive scale of public events, they offer the illusion of the intimate space of the human voice—and they do so in a poem that has already interrogated our need to hear voices where there are none: *you are not alone.*

Glück is bold enough to honor the great recuperative mission of poetry: when she says "I am / at work," isolating the two syllables "I am" on the line, she inevitably invokes Coleridge's definition of the imagination in the *Biographia Literaria.* But she also says that when she is at work she is silent; no one can hear her. The little book of poems read on the subway train not only goes unnamed, its content is unmentioned, beside the point. The wonder of poetry in "October" is the wonder of the stars: they "give nothing but ask nothing."

To want more than that is to want something other than poetry. And if we are disheartened by such consolation, we are also ennobled. For as *The Winter's Tale* suggests, poetry's greatest power is to instill in us a craving for something other than poetry: the person, not the statue, is the wonder. This is why a poem content with its own wisdom could not console us for long. We want to feel poetry turning against itself again and again—not only because we need to interrogate our best ideas but because we want to experience the sensation, the sound, of words leaping just beyond our capacity to know them certainly. We live in unexpected detours of syntax, the exfoliating connotations of metaphor.

So while a poem might speak vividly in one circumstance, it may never speak again. An event of unimaginable proportion may render a poem shockingly relevant, or it may make the poem feel smaller than ever before: a little book in a big world. In any case, the power of a poem inheres in the realization that we cannot count on it. Its ephemeral consolation depends precisely on its being ephemeral, open to the vicissitudes of self-doubt. Not wonder, but composed wonder. Not the composition achieved, but the composition unraveling. Not the meaning as such but the fact of the poem's existence as a movement of language—small enough to be remembered whole, difficult enough to be forgotten. "From within earth's / bitter disgrace, coldness and barrenness," says the poem, "my friend the moon rises: / she is beautiful tonight, but when is she not beautiful?" The wonder is our resistance to it.

BIBLIOGRAPHY

THE RESISTANCE TO POETRY

Auden, W. H. "In Memory of W. B. Yeats." In *The English Auden,* edited
    by Edward Mendelson, pp. 241–43. New York: Random House,
    1977.

Callimachus. "Prologue to the *Aetia.*" In *Hymns, Epigrams, Select Fragments,*
    pp. 65–66. Translated by Stanley Lombardo and Diane Rayor. Baltimore:
    Johns Hopkins University Press, 1988.

Dante Alighieri. "Canto XXVI." In *The Inferno,* pp. 270–79. Translated by
    Robert Pinsky. New York: Farrar, Straus & Giroux, 1994.

Dickinson, Emily. "Best Things dwell out of Sight." In *The Manuscript Books,*
    edited by R. W. Franklin, 2:1225. 2 vols. Cambridge, Mass.: Harvard
    University Press, 1981.

————. "Best Things dwell out of Sight." In *The Poems: Variorum Edition,*
    edited by R. W. Franklin, 2:905. 3 vols. Cambridge, Mass.: Harvard
    University Press, 1998.

————. "Going—to—Her!" In *The Poems: Variorum Edition,* edited by R. W.
    Franklin, 1:294–95. 3 vols. Cambridge, Mass.: Harvard University Press,
    1998.

————. Letter to Thomas Higginson, 7 June 1862. In *The Letters,* edited by
    Thomas H. Johnson and Theodora Ward, 2:408–9. 3 vols. Cambridge,
    Mass.: Harvard University Press, 1958.

Hardy, Thomas. Notebook entry, 17 October 1896. In *The Life and Work of
    Thomas Hardy,* edited by Michael Milgate, p. 302. London: Macmillan,
    1984.

Horace. "Epistle ii.1: To Augustus." In *The Epistles,* pp. 111–31. Translated by
    David Ferry. New York: Farrar, Straus & Giroux, 2001.

Howard, Richard. "Poetry: Our Worst-Kept Secret." *Harper's* 294 (April 1997): 27–30.

Levi, Primo. *If This Is a Man.* Translated by Stuart Woolf. London: Orion, 1960.

Mandelstam, Nadezhda. "The Path to Destruction." In *Hope against Hope: A Memoir,* pp. 157–62. Translated by Max Hayward. New York: Athenaeum, 1970.

Mandelstam, Osip. "[The Stalin Epigram.]" In *Selected Poems,* pp. 69–70. Translated by Clarence Brown and W. S. Merwin. London: Oxford University Press, 1973.

Moore, Marianne. Letter to Ezra Pound, 9 January 1919. In *The Selected Letters,* edited by Bonnie Costello, pp. 122–25. New York: Knopf, 1997.

————. "Marriage." In *The Complete Poems,* pp. 62–70. New York: Viking, 1967.

Mullen, Harryette. *Muse & Drudge.* Philadelphia: Singing Horse Press, 1995.

Pinsky, Robert. "The People's Verse." *New York Times,* 10 April 1997, A:29.

Pound, Ezra. "Homage to Sextus Propertius." In *Personae,* edited by Lea Baechler and A. Walton Litz, pp. 205–24. New York: New Directions, 1990.

Virgil. "Eclogue VI." In *The Eclogues,* pp. 45–51. Translated by David Ferry. New York: Farrar, Straus & Giroux, 1999.

Whitman, Walt. "Crossing Brooklyn Ferry." In *Leaves of Grass,* edited by Harold Blodgett and Scully Bradley, pp. 159–65. New York: Norton, 1965.

Winnicott, D. W. "Communicating and Not Communicating Leading to a Study of Certain Opposites." In *The Maturational Processes and the Facilitating Environment,* pp. 179–92. New York: International Universities Press, 1965.

Yeats, W. B. "On Being Asked for a War Poem." In *The Poems,* edited by Richard J. Finneran, pp. 155–56. New York: Macmillan, 1989.

————. "A Packet for Ezra Pound." In *A Vision,* pp. 3–30. New York: Macmillan, 1956.

THE END OF THE LINE

Bidart, Frank. "The Second Hour of the Night." In *Desire,* pp. 27–59. New York: Farrar, Straus & Giroux, 1997.

Cunningham, J. V. "How Shall the Poem Be Written?" In *Collected Essays,* pp. 256–71. Chicago: Swallow Press, 1976.

Frost, Robert. "After Apple Picking." In *Collected Poems, Prose, and Plays,* edited by Richard Poirier and Mark Richardson, pp. 70–71. New York: Library of America, 1995.

Hollander, John. " 'Sense Variously Drawn Out': On English Enjambment." In *Vision and Resonance: Two Senses of Poetic Form,* pp. 91–116. New York: Oxford University Press, 1975.

Jarrell, Randall. "The End of the Line." In *Kipling, Auden & Co.,* pp. 76–83. New York: Farrar, Straus & Giroux, 1980.

Johnson, Samuel. "Milton." In *Lives of the English Poets,* edited by George Birkbeck Hill, 1:84–194. 3 Vols. Oxford: Clarendon Press, 1905.

Justice, Donald. "The Free-Verse Line in Stevens." In *Oblivion: On Writers and Writing,* pp. 13–38. Ashland, Oreg.: Story Line, 1998.

Milton, John. *Paradise Lost.* In *Complete Poems and Major Prose,* edited by Merritt Hughes, pp. 209–469. Indianapolis: Odyssey, 1957.

Moore, Marianne. "The Accented Syllable." In *The Complete Prose,* edited by Patricia Willis, pp. 31–34. New York: Viking, 1986.

———. "The Fish." *Egoist* 5 (August 1918): 95.

———. "The Fish." In *Others for 1919,* edited by Alfred Kreymborg, pp. 125–27. New York: Nicholas Brown, 1920.

Pound, Ezra. "Canto IV." In *The Cantos,* pp. 13–16. New York: New Directions, 1975.

———. "Harold Monro." *Criterion* 11 (July 1932): 581–92.

Shakespeare, William. *King Lear.* Edited by Kenneth Muir. London: Methuen, 1975.

Stevens, Wallace. "The Snow Man." In *The Collected Poems,* pp. 9–10. New York: Knopf, 1954.

Williams, William Carlos. "Pastoral." In *The Collected Poems.* Vol. 1, *1909–1939,* edited by A. Walton Litz and Christopher MacGowan, pp. 64–65. New York: New Directions, 1986.

———. *Spring and All.* In *The Collected Poems.* Vol. 1, *1909–1939,* edited by A. Walton Litz and Christopher MacGowan, pp. 177–236. New York: New Directions, 1986.

———. "To a Poor Old Woman." In *The Collected Poems.* Vol. 1, *1909–1939,* edited by A. Walton Litz and Christopher MacGowan, p. 383. New York: New Directions, 1986.

FORMS OF DISJUNCTION

Ashbery, John. "Notes from the Air." In *Hotel Lautréamont,* pp. 11–12. New York: Knopf, 1992.

Auden, W. H. "Foreword." In *Some Trees,* by John Ashbery, pp. 11–16. New Haven, Conn.: Yale University Press, 1956.

———. Letter to Frank O'Hara, 3 June 1955. In *City Poet: The Life and Times of Frank O'Hara,* by Brad Gooch, p. 261. New York: Knopf, 1993.

Eliot, T. S. "Gerontion." In *The Complete Poems and Plays,* pp. 21–23. New York: Harcourt, 1971.

———. "The Love Song of J. Alfred Prufrock." In *The Complete Poems and Plays,* pp. 3–7. New York: Harcourt, 1971.

———. *The Waste Land.* In *The Complete Poems and Plays,* pp. 37–55. New York: Harcourt, 1971.

Frost, Robert. "Directive." In *Collected Poems, Prose, and Plays,* edited by Richard Poirier and Mark Richardson, pp. 341–42. New York: Library of America, 1995.

Graham, Jorie. "Le Manteau de Pascal." In *The Errancy,* pp. 64–70. Hopewell, N.J.: Ecco, 1997.

Koethe, John. "The Constructor." In *The Constructor,* pp. 43–49. New York: HarperCollins, 1999.

Pound, Ezra. "Canto II." In *The Cantos,* pp. 6–10. New York: New Directions, 1975.

Stein, Gertrude. "Sentences." In *How to Write,* pp.113–213. New York: Dover, 1975.

Walcott, Derek. "Map of the New World." In *Collected Poems, 1948–1984,* pp. 413–17. New York: Farrar, Straus & Giroux, 1986.

Waldrop, Rosmarie. *A Key into the Language of America.* New York: New Directions, 1994.

Wordsworth, William. "The Two-Part *Prelude* of 1799." In *The Prelude 1799, 1805, 1850,* edited by Jonathan Wordsworth, M. H. Abrams, and Stephen Gill, pp. 1–27. New York: Norton, 1979.

Wright, Charles. "Indian Summer II." In *Negative Blue: Selected Later Poems,* p. 163. New York: Farrar, Straus & Giroux, 2000.

———. "Stray Paragraphs in April, Year of the Rat." In *Negative Blue: Selected Later Poems,* p. 146. New York: Farrar, Straus & Giroux, 2000.

Wright, James. "Lying in a Hammock at William Duffy's Farm in Pine Island, Minnesota." In *Above the River: The Complete Poems,* p. 122. New York: Farrar, Straus & Giroux, 1990.

Yeats, W. B. "Politics." In *The Poems,* edited by Richard J. Finneran, p. 348. New York: Macmillan, 1989.

Bernstein, Charles. "The Artifice of Absorption." In *A Poetics*, pp. 9–81. Cambridge, Mass.: Harvard University Press, 1992.

———. "Empty Biscuits." In *With Strings*, p. 69. Chicago: University of Chicago Press, 2001.

———. "Johnny Cake Hollow." In *With Strings*, p. 27. Chicago: University of Chicago Press, 2001.

———. "Poem." In *With Strings*, pp. 20–21. Chicago: University of Chicago Press, 2001.

———. "Today's Not Opposite Day." In *With Strings*, pp. 72–77. Chicago: University of Chicago Press, 2001.

Burns, Robert. "Auld Lang Syne." In *Poems and Songs*, edited by James Kinsley, pp. 353–54. New York: Oxford University Press, 1969.

Dickens, Charles. *David Copperfield*. Edited by Jerome H. Buckley. New York: Norton, 1990.

Oppen, George. "Debt." In *New Collected Poems*, edited by Michael Davidson, p. 60. New York: New Directions, 2002.

———. Letter to Max and Anita Pepper, 12 June 1962. In *The Selected Letters*, edited by Rachel Blau DuPlessis, pp. 62–66. Durham, N.C.: Duke University Press, 1990.

———. "The Manufactured Part." In *New Collected Poems*, edited by Michael Davidson, pp. 366–67. New York: New Directions, 2002.

———. "Psalm." In *New Collected Poems*, edited by Michael Davidson, p. 99. New York: New Directions, 2002.

Silliman, Ron. "Third Phase Objectivism." In *The New Sentence*, pp. 136–41. New York: Roof, 1987.

Voigt, Ellen Bryant. "The Art of Distance." In *Shadow of Heaven*, pp. 45–60. New York: Norton, 2002.

Zukofsky, Louis. "Sincerity and Objectification." *Poetry* 37 (1931): 272–85.

UNTIDY ACTIVITY

Auden, W. H. "Foreword." In *A Change of World*, by Adrienne Cecile Rich, pp. 7–11. New Haven, Conn.: Yale University Press, 1951.

Baudelaire, Charles. "Correspondences." In *Les Fleurs du Mal*, p. 15. Translated by Richard Howard. Boston: Godine, 1983.

Bishop, Elizabeth. "The Bight." In *The Complete Poems*, pp. 60–61. New York: Farrar, Straus & Giroux, 1980.

————. "The 'Darwin' Letter." In *Elizabeth Bishop and Her Art,* edited by Lloyd Schwartz and Sybil P. Estess, p. 288. Ann Arbor: University of Michigan Press, 1983.

Emerson, Ralph Waldo. "The Poet." In *Essays and Lectures,* edited by Joel Porte, pp. 445–68. New York: Library of America, 1983.

Palmer, Michael. "Baudelaire Series." In *Codes Appearing: Poems 1979–1988,* pp. 163–96. New York: New Directions, 2001.

————. "Notes for Echo Lake 1." In *Codes Appearing: Poems 1979–1988,* pp. 4–6. New York: New Directions, 2001.

————. "Seven Poems within a Matrix for War." In *At Passages,* pp. 13–26. New York: New Directions, 1995.

Poirier, Richard. "Resistance in Itself." In *The Renewal of Literature: Emersonian Reflections,* pp. 135–81. New York: Random House, 1987.

Pound, Ezra. "Canto LXXXIII." In *The Cantos,* pp. 528–36. New York: New Directions, 1975.

Rich, Adrienne. "An Atlas of the Difficult World V." In *An Atlas of the Difficult World: Poems 1988–1991,* pp. 12–13. New York: Norton, 1991.

————. Foreword to *Collected Early Poems: 1950–1970,* pp. xix–xxi. New York: Norton, 1993.

Stevens, Wallace. "Nuances of a Theme by Williams." In *The Collected Poems,* p. 18. New York: Knopf, 1954.

Strand, Mark. "The Untelling" In *The Story of Our Lives,* pp. 38–48. New York: Athenaeum, 1973.

Williams, William Carlos. "El Hombre." In *The Collected Poems.* Vol. 1, *1909–1936,* edited by A. Walton Litz and Christopher MacGowan, p. 76. New York: New Directions, 1986.

Winnicott, D. W. "Ego Distortion in Terms of True and False Self." In *The Maturational Processes and the Facilitating Environment,* pp. 140–52. New York: International Universities Press, 1965.

THE SPOKENNESS OF POETRY

Bakhtin, Mikhail. *The Dialogic Imagination.* Translated by Caryl Emerson and Michael Holquist. Austin: University of Texas Press, 1981.

Bidart, Frank. "The Yoke." In *Desire,* p. 14. New York: Farrar, Straus & Giroux, 1997.

Browning, Robert. "Essay on Shelley." In *The Poetical Works,* edited by Ian Jack, 4:424–42. 8 vols. Oxford: Clarendon Press, 1991.

———. "Fra Lippo Lippi." In *The Poetical Works,* edited by Ian Jack, 5:35–53. 8 vols. Oxford: Clarendon Press, 1995.

Cioran, E. M. "On Being Lyrical." In *On the Heights of Despair,* pp. 3–5. Translated by Ilinca Zarifopol-Johnston. Chicago: University of Chicago Press, 1992.

Crane, Hart. "Repose of Rivers." In *Complete Poems,* edited by Marc Simon, p. 16. New York: Liveright, 1986.

Donne, John. "The Canonization." In *The Complete Poetry,* edited by John T. Shawcross, pp. 96–97. Garden City, N.Y.: Anchor, 1967.

Eliot, T. S. "The Love Song of J. Alfred Prufrock." In *The Complete Poems and Plays,* pp. 3–7. New York: Harcourt, 1971.

Frost, Robert. "Preface to 'A Way Out.' " In *Collected Poems, Prose, and Plays,* edited by Richard Poirier and Mark Richardson, p. 713. New York: Library of America, 1995.

Glück, Louise. "Castile." In *Vita Nova,* pp. 27–28. Hopewell, N.J.: Ecco, 1999.

———. "Clover." In *The Wild Iris,* p. 30. Hopewell, N.J.: Ecco, 1992.

———. "Daisies." In *The Wild Iris,* p. 39. Hopewell, N.J.: Ecco, 1992.

———. "Retreating Wind." In *The Wild Iris,* p. 15. Hopewell, N.J.: Ecco, 1992.

———. "Scilla." In *The Wild Iris,* p. 14. Hopewell, N.J.: Ecco, 1992.

———. "The Wild Iris." In *The Wild Iris,* p. 1. Hopewell, N.J.: Ecco, 1992.

Hammer, Langdon. "Frank Bidart and the Tone of Contemporary Poetry." *Southwest Review* 87 (2002): 75–89.

Langbaum, Robert. *The Poetry of Experience: The Dramatic Monologue in Modern Literary Tradition.* New York: Norton, 1957.

Pound, Ezra. "Vorticism." In *Gaudier-Brzeska,* pp. 81–94. New York: New Directions, 1970.

Tennyson, Alfred. "Ulysses." In *The Poems,* edited by Christopher Ricks, pp. 560–66. London: Longmans, 1969.

Wordsworth, William. "Note to 'The Thorn.' " In *Lyrical Ballads, and Other Poems, 1797–1800,* edited by James Butler and Karen Green, pp. 350–51. Ithaca, N.Y.: Cornell University Press, 1992.

Yeats, W. B. "Sailing to Byzantium." In *The Poems,* edited by Richard J. Finneran, pp. 193–94. New York: Macmillan, 1989.

THE OTHER HAND

Auden, W. H. "September 1, 1939." In *The English Auden,* edited by Edward Mendelson, pp. 245–47. New York: Random House, 1977.

Eliot, T. S. "The Love Song of J. Alfred Prufrock." In *The Complete Poems and Plays,* pp. 3–7. New York: Harcourt, 1971.

Oppen, George. "Of Being Numerous." In *New Collected Poems,* edited by Michael Davidson, pp. 163–188. New York: New Directions, 2002.

———. "A Theological Definition." In *New Collected Poems,* edited by Michael Davidson, p. 203. New York: New Directions, 2002.

———. "Till Other Voices Wake Us." In *New Collected Poems,* edited by Michael Davidson, p. 286. New York: New Directions, 2002.

Phillips, Carl. "The Clearing." In *Rock Harbor,* pp. 20–22. New York: Farrar, Straus & Giroux, 2002.

———. "Golden." In *Rock Harbor,* pp. 3–4. New York: Farrar, Straus & Giroux, 2002.

———. "The Pinnacle." In *The Tether,* pp. 61–65. New York: Farrar, Straus & Giroux, 2001.

———. "Stagger." In *The Tether,* pp. 25–26. New York: Farrar, Straus & Giroux, 2001.

Pound, Ezra. "Canto I." In *The Cantos,* pp. 3–5. New York: New Directions, 1975.

———. "Canto VIII." In *The Cantos,* pp. 28–33. New York: New Directions, 1975.

Proust, Marcel. *Within a Budding Grove.* Translated by C. K. Scott Moncrieff and Terence Kilmartin. Revised by D. J. Enright. New York: Modern Library, 1992.

Shakespeare, William. *Antony and Cleopatra.* Edited by John Wilders. London: Routledge, 1995.

———. *Hamlet.* Edited by Harold Jenkins. London: Methuen, 1982.

Stevens, Wallace. "Notes toward a Supreme Fiction." In *The Collected Poems,* pp. 380–408. New York: Knopf, 1954.

Wittgenstein, Ludwig. *Philosophical Investigations.* Translated by G. E. M. Anscombe. Englewood Cliffs, N.J.: Prentice Hall, 1953.

LEAVING THINGS OUT

Bishop, Elizabeth. "Cape Breton." In *The Complete Poems,* pp. 67–68. New York: Farrar, Straus & Giroux, 1980.

Bradley, A. C. " 'He Has No Children.' " In *Shakespearean Tragedy,* pp. 398–401. New York: Meridian, 1955.

Dickinson, Emily. "I cannot live with You." In *The Poems: Variorum Edition,*

edited by R. W. Franklin, 2:674–76. 3 vols. Cambridge, Mass.: Harvard
    University Press, 1998.

Freud, Sigmund. *The Interpretation of Dreams.* In *The Standard Edition of the
    Complete Psychological Works,* edited and translated by James Strachey,
    vols. 4–5. 24 vols. London: Hogarth, 1958.

Graham, Jorie. "For One Must Want / To Shut the Other's Gaze." In *Swarm,* pp.
    55–56. New York: Ecco, 2000.

———. *"from* The Reformation Journal." In *Swarm,* pp. 3–5. New York: Ecco,
    2000.

———. "Gulls." In *Never,* pp. 26–30. New York: Ecco, 2002.

———. "Le Manteau de Pascal." In *The Errancy,* pp. 64–70. Hopewell, N.J.:
    Ecco, 1997.

———. "Prayer." In *Never,* p. 3. New York: Ecco, 2002.

———. "Untitled Two." In *The Errancy,* pp. 25–27. Hopewell, N.J.: Ecco,
    1997.

Hemingway, Ernest. "Hunger was Good Discipline." In *A Moveable Feast,* pp.
    69–77. New York: Scribner, 1964.

Levinson, Marjorie. "Insight and Oversight: Reading 'Tintern Abbey.'" In
    Wordsworth's Great Period Poems, pp. 14–57. New York: Cambridge
    University Press, 1986.

McGann, Jerome. "Wordsworth and the Ideology of Romantic Poems." In *The
    Romantic Ideology,* pp. 81–92. Chicago: University of Chicago Press, 1983.

Shakespeare, William. *The Merchant of Venice.* Edited by John Russell Brown.
    London: Methuen, 1961.

Stevens, Wallace. "Notes toward a Supreme Fiction." In *The Collected Poems,* pp.
    380–408. New York: Knopf, 1954.

———. "Responses to *Partisan Review* Questionnaire." In *Opus Posthumous,*
    edited by Milton Bates, pp. 308–10. New York: Knopf, 1989.

Virgil. "Eclogue IX." In *The Eclogues,* pp. 71–77. Translated by David Ferry. New
    York: Farrar, Straus & Giroux, 1999.

Wordsworth, William. "Lines written a few miles above Tintern Abbey." In
    Lyrical Ballads, and Other Poems, 1797–1800, edited by James Butler and
    Karen Green, pp. 116–20. Ithaca, N.Y.: Cornell University Press, 1992.

COMPOSED WONDER

Aristotle. *Metaphysics.* In *The Complete Works of Aristotle: The Revised Oxford
    Translation,* edited by Jonathan Barnes, 2:1552–1728. 2 vols. Princeton,
    N.J.: Princeton University Press, 1984.

————. *Rhetoric*. In *The Complete Works of Aristotle: The Revised Oxford Translation,* edited by Jonathan Barnes, 2:2152–269. 2 vols. Princeton, N.J.: Princeton University Press, 1984.

Cioran, E. M. "The Fall Out of Time." In *The Fall into Time,* pp. 173–83. Translated by Richard Howard. Chicago: Quadrangle Books, 1970.

Cunningham, J. V. "Wonder." In *Collected Essays,* pp. 53–96. Chicago: Swallow Press, 1976.

Fisher, Phillip. *Wonder, the Rainbow, and the Aesthetics of Rare Experiences.* Cambridge, Mass.: Harvard University Press, 1998.

Ford, Ford Madox. *No More Parades.* In *Parade's End,* pp. 291–500. New York: Vintage, 1979.

Glück, Louise. "Nostos." In *Meadowlands,* p. 43. Hopewell, N.J.: Ecco, 1996.

————. "October." *The New Yorker* 78 (28 October 2002): 92–93.

————. "Solstice." In *The Seven Ages,* p. 10. New York: Ecco, 2001.

Hecht, Anthony. " 'It Out-Herods Herod. Pray You, Avoid It.' " In *The Hard Hours,* pp. 67–68. New York: Atheneum, 1975.

Phillips, Adam. "Smile." In *Promises, Promises,* pp. 181–87. London: Faber & Faber, 2000.

Shakespeare, William. *Hamlet.* Edited by Harold Jenkins. London: Methuen, 1982.

————. *Shakespeare's Sonnets.* Edited by Stephen Booth. New Haven, Conn.: Yale University Press, 1977.

————. *The Tempest.* Edited by Frank Kermode. London: Methuen, 1969.

————. *The Winter's Tale.* Edited by J. H. P. Pafford. London: Methuen, 1966.

Woolf, Virginia. *To the Lighthouse.* New York: Harcourt, 1955.

INDEX